DYNAMIC STUDIES IN ROMANS

BRINGING GOD'S WORD TO LIFE

FRED A. SCHEEREN

WESTBOW®
PRESS
A DIVISION OF THOMAS NELSON
& ZONDERVAN

WestBow Press books may be ordered through booksellers or by contacting:

WestBow Press
A Division of Thomas Nelson & Zondervan
1663 Liberty Drive
Bloomington, IN 47403
www.westbowpress.com
1 (866) 928-1240

ISBN: 978-1-4908-4049-9 (sc)
ISBN: 978-1-4908-4050-5 (e)

Library of Congress Control Number: 2014910658

Printed in the United States of America.

WestBow Press rev. date: 07/15/2014

I DEDICATE THIS book to my lovely wife, Sally, who is a Jewish believer. She has stood by me over the years and raised our sons in a God-loving home. The comfort of sharing our friendship and love for Christ has encouraged me greatly in creating this series of dynamic studies of various books of the Bible. Sally's participation in our small group studies has added a much deeper dimension of richness to the discussions. Thank you for sharing your heritage, training, and knowledge.

CONTENTS

PREFACE

WELCOME TO MY study guide for one of the most remarkable documents in the course of human history, the Book of Romans----which is a part of the Judeo Christian documents which we now call the Bible. I hope that you will find this to be a worthy and most enjoyable study.

As we consider how this book fits into the whole of the New Testament documents and the Tanakh (Tanakh, the name used for the Old Testament by the Jews, is used here to emphasize the Jewishness of the Scriptures.) we need to realize a number of things. We need to stand in awe of this overall combination of 66 books, written over thousands of years by at least 40 different authors. Every detail of the text is there by design. It explains history before it happens and comes to us from outside the dimension of time. It is, in short, the most amazing, most authenticated, and most accurate book available in the world.

If this claim is not strong enough, add to it the indisputable fact that the words contained therein have changed more lives than any others now in existence.

And now back to this particular study.

This particular group of studies was originally meant to be used in a Small Group setting. However, it can also be adapted to a larger group or individual study.

You will notice that in most instances I have included the citation, but not the actual text, of the portion of scripture that we are considering at any point in time. This is on purpose. I believe that we all learn more effectively if we have to dig out the text itself. As a byproduct of that exercise we all become more familiar with this marvelous book.

You will also notice that the scripture references are preceded by or followed by a question or series of questions. Again, this is on purpose. I have also found that people seem to learn most effectively when employing the "Socratic Method." That is instead of telling someone what the text says and how it relates to other texts and life, they will remember it much more completely if they answer questions about it and ferret the information out for themselves.

While the subject of our study, the Judeo Christian Scriptures, are demonstrably perfect, my prepared studies are not. There is no way that I, or anyone else, could possibly incorporate the depth of the text into individual sessions. Many people have written volumes on one chapter of Romans alone. I simply desire to provide a vehicle for others to use in their investigation of the scriptures as they incorporate these timeless truths into their lives.

One perfect example of the depth of the book of Romans and the impossibility of capturing it all at one time comes from an interesting experience I had when putting these sessions together. One Saturday morning I was trying to prepare several sessions at one sitting. By the time I finished the third session I was mentally exhausted. About a month later when it came time to present the third session I forgot that I had already prepared it. So, I spent two more hours getting the study ready again. When I realized my mistake I compared the two sessions and was surprised to find that they were very different. One person studying the same material utilizing the same resources got two very different lessons out of it. This will happen time and again as we continue to plumb the depths of The Word.

ACKNOWLEDGEMENTS

I WANT TO acknowledge my friend, Bob Mason, who was at this writing in his second career as the Pastor of Small Groups at the Bible Chapel in the South Hills of Pittsburgh, is responsible for the overall structure of each session. Realizing that our group was doing somewhat more in-depth work than most, he asked that I be sure to include several important segments in each session, most specifically the warm up phase and the life application phase.

One of the great resources for this, as suggested by Bob, is the now out of print New Testament Lesson Planner from Intervarsity Press. I have augmented this with commentaries by Chuck Missler from Koinonia House, as well as the whole of scripture itself. In order to make the utilization of the whole of scripture more efficient, I have also leaned heavily on the Libronix Digital Library, which is perhaps the most advanced Bible software available. This is only a partial list as I have utilized a number of other resources to help us understand how the New Testament and the Tanakh fit together as one cohesive document.

One of the things that helped make my work easier in preparing this material was the periodic lists of cross references sent to me by my friend Dr. David Fink. David continued to send me cross references for any chapter of the scriptures in question so that I could weave them into the discussion as appropriate so long as his health permitted.

Additionally, I would like to acknowledge the members of our Small Group Bible Study, with whom I first reviewed and utilized this material. This fine group of diverse people has grown closer together as a result of our regular meetings and we have seen some miraculous things happen in each other's lives. Our members at the time of the initial study included:

- Alison Chunko, a business owner who was healed of a deadly lung disease during the course of our studies;

- Cathy Harvey, a high school teacher and dog breeder who was also healed of a serious eye disorder during our the course of our studies;

- Dan Chunko, a criminal attorney who also handled the keyboards for the Bible Chapel (Dan is the only person I know who can play three keyboards at one time);

- Dr. David Fink, a former professor of Greek and pastor;

- Joyce Smith Fink, former assistant to the President at Pittsburgh Theological Seminary;

- Scott Swart, former marine with a White House security clearance and currently involved with the Washington City Mission;

- Wendy Swart, a business owner and operator;

- Bob McDemas, Metallurgist and business owner;

- Kim McDemas, owner of an international company specializing in strategic planning for corporations;

- Ron Carrola, a well-known Transportation Engineer;

- Felicia Carrola, who was fully engaged home schooling her several children, one of whom composed full orchestral scores while still in high school and another of whom published his first book also while still in high school;

- Vonnie Teagarden, a psychotherapist in private practice;

- Tom Nicastro, the local service manager for a major international corporation;

- Cindy Nicastro, a Physical Therapist with many years of expertise and experience; and

- Sally Scheeren, my wife, an accomplished private practice attorney, and her brother Joey, a successful real estate developer, who became a believer during the course of our studies.

(I thank you all.)

As you read through the roster of the people in this particular, small group, you can see my good fortune to study with so many well-read, intelligent, and successful people. The group, of course, was not by accident. God's plan is greater than any we can imagine and His caring for us certainly includes the makeup of any small group devoted to the study of His Word. I believe that every such small group convened for this purpose will have a mix of participants that is similarly suited to enhance the growth and learning of the group members individually and the group as a whole.

And finally, speaking of small groups, I'd like to acknowledge Dr. Chuck Missler, a former fortune 500 CEO, who claims that this is where he experienced the greatest growth in his life as a believer. I trust that you may find this to be true in your experience and encourage you to be an active participant in such a mutually supportive, biblically-based group.

INTRODUCTION:
GROUND RULES

I DESIGNED THE first portion of each study to encourage everyone to think about their personal situation and to get them personally involved. The second portion is designed to help us understand what the text says and how it relates to the whole of Scripture. And finally, each session ends with a discussion intended to help those present apply that day's lesson to their lives.

You will notice that in most instances I have included the citation, but not the actual text of the portion of Scripture that we are considering. This is on purpose. I believe that we all learn more effectively if we have to dig out the text itself. As a byproduct of that exercise, we all become more familiar with this marvelous book.

You will also notice that the scripture references are preceded by or followed by a question or series of questions. Again, this is on purpose. I have also found that people seem to learn most effectively when employing the "Socratic Method." That is, instead of telling someone what the text says and how it relates to other texts and life, they will remember it much more completely if they answer questions about it and ferret the information out for themselves.

In a few instances, I have inserted additional commentary or partial answers to some of the questions being discussed in order to help the group get the greatest possible good out of the study.

In addition, I have added various scriptural references intending that they be read out loud as part of the session. Shorter passages might be read by one participant, while anything over two or three verses might serve everyone better if one member reads one verse and another reads the next until the passage is completed. This keeps everyone involved and on the same page. After reading these passages, I intend that they be seriously considered as they relate to the primary scripture at hand in Romans. At times, this relationship seems to be available and obvious on the surface. In many other instances, the interconnectedness of the whole of scripture and its principles are most effectively understood through deeper thought, discussion, and prayer along the way.

In commenting on and discussing the various scriptures, questions, concepts, and principles in this material it is not required that any particular person give their particular input. The reader of any passage may, but is not required to give their thoughts to the group. This is a group participation exercise for the mutual benefit of all involved and many people in the group giving their insight into a certain passage or question will often enhance the learning experience. I also have two very practical suggestions if you do this in a small-group setting. Every time you meet, review the calendar and go over meetings scheduled for the future and establish who will bring refreshments. This just makes things run a lot better while enhancing everyone's enjoyment and expectations.

My guess is that you will find going through this material enjoyable and helpful. You will likely find it even more enjoyable if you have the privilege of going through it with a small group of believers such as I have been privileged to do. I know I have enjoyed going through these studies and feel as though I have gotten more out of the experience than I would have if I had only engaged in the study by myself.

May God bless you, inspire you, teach you, and change your life for the better as you go through these sessions.

Background to the Book of Romans

ABOUT 500 BC Socrates said to Plato "It may be that deity can forgive sins, but I do not see how." The inherent problem with this dilemma is that it is impossible for a holy and just deity to forgive sins without acting counter to his nature.

The God of the Bible, however, had a solution to this problem that to a human mind seemed insurmountable. That solution was God's grace. We have all seen the acronym that describes this.

God's'

Riches

At

Christ's

Expense

The problems inherent to the dilemma put forth by the Greek philosophers became apparent during the dark ages in Europe from about 590 to 1517. During this period of time, we saw the understanding of God's Grace enjoyed by the early believers erode into forms of legalism.

This brought us to the Reformation.

In 1483 in Eisleben, Saxony a baby boy was born to a poor coal miner. Having watched his parents live in poverty, this young man, named Martin, decided to become a lawyer. He attended the University of Erfurt where he was a top student.

In 1504, a thunderstorm so violent that it almost scared him to death, broke out when he was walking across campus. He instinctively called out to the patron saint of coal miners, Saint Anne, and said "If you save me from this storm I will become a monk."

Martin lived through the storm and fulfilled his promise to become a monk. In this role he found no peace since he held to a form of religion without substance. While on a pilgrimage across the Alps, he almost died. He was rescued by a monk who knew about true Peace and Grace and suggested that he read the book of Habakkuk.

This ultimately led this man, who we know as Martin Luther, to find God's grace which fueled his efforts and which became the beginning of the reformation.

Many people at that time then returned to God's word, and found true Grace and Peace.

This leads us to the theme of Romans, which is God's grace revealed. Many scholars have called Romans the most profound book of all literature. For many people this is the most important book in the New Testament.

As we begin our review of the marvelous book of Romans we should again remind ourselves that it is part of an integrated message system, which we call the Bible, that comes to us from outside the boundaries of time and space. Every detail, every place name, every form of punctuation is there by design. In a human sense, it was written by at least 40 authors over thousands of years and fits together in ways more perfect than we can comprehend.

As we review the book of Romans and see how it fits into the whole of Scripture, we will, with the help of the Holy Spirit, be astounded at the depth of the writing and the grace of our Creator.

It has often been said, "If God were small enough for our minds he wouldn't be big enough for our needs." In fact, this statement has become so well-known and accepted that it has almost achieved the status of a proverb. While the statement itself incorporates well-known Scriptural principles, we don't actually know who first said it in this succinct and impactful fashion. Suffice it to say that whoever it was knew the Scriptures and also seems to have been well acquainted with their Author. We will become even more aware of the truth of this statement during the time we spend in Romans, as we ask God to open our minds and teach us from the His Word.

WEEK 1

AN INTRODUCTION
ROMANS 1:1-7

Opening Prayer

Group Warm-Up Question

If you were writing a first letter to a pen pal, how would you introduce yourself?

- What would you tell them about yourself?

- What would you tell them about the purpose of the letter?

- Why would you do this is such a fashion?

- What would you be trying to accomplish?

Scriptural Overview for us to Consider:
Read: Habakkuk 2:4

      Romans 1:17

      Galatians 3:11

      Hebrews 10:39

How might one summarize these verses?

Read Romans 1:1-7 with a different person reading each verse.

How did Paul introduce and identify himself to the Romans?

What special calling did Paul feel on his life?

Paul liked the term "servant." The Greek word he used for this was *doulos*, meaning "bond slave." Read Exodus 21:2-6 to understand what a bond slave is.

The mark of a bond slave was a mark of honor. We should also understand that a slave of someone in a high position had more status, authority, and freedom than a free commoner. The emperor's slaves were some of the highest-ranking people in the empire.

Read Galatians 1:10 and comment.

Read Titus 1:1 and comment.

If Paul was a bond slave of Jesus Christ, what does this infer about his position?

Note: It is also instructive to note that once a bond slave was adopted into a family, that slave could never be disowned.

What does this infer about our position with God and the assurance we can have?

When was Paul called or Chosen?
Read: Acts 9:1-19

> Jeremiah 1:5

> Ephesians 1:3-4

When did God begin to work in your life?

Read John 12:32 and comment.
Think back again to Romans 1:1-7

In what ways does Paul say God has revealed himself to people?

To which part of the Bible was he referring?

Who is the focus of God's gospel?

What credentials does Jesus have to confirm his claim as the son of God?

Read Acts 10:43. We can see Jesus Christ on every page of the New and Old Testament. Paul also calls himself an apostle. What does this mean?

Read: Matthew 10:1-2

     1 Corinthians 9:1

     Acts 9:15

     Galatians 1:1

     Galatians 2:7-9

What specific calling did Paul and others receive on their lives?

Who was the new group of people being exposed to the Gospel message?

Why was this new to them?

What were/are people called to believe?

Read 1 Corinthians 15:1-9.

In the context of our discussion, to believe means personally to trust.

What is the result of this belief?

How did Paul describe the people who were receiving his letter?

Vitally Important Question: In what way do you feel God has placed a special calling on your life? (Go around the group so that each person has the opportunity to answer.)

Consider the words you use to describe yourself to others as a follower of Jesus Christ? This is important. Do you call yourself a believer? A Christian? Why?

What is the effect of this?

Note: God will give us the wisdom we need in such discussions if we ask Him for it, as well as for the filling of His Holy Spirit.

Make Learning Attractive.

Read Proverbs 16:21 in several versions.

What do most people today believe about God's plan for their salvation or eternal destiny?

How have your beliefs changed about Jesus Christ during the various stages of your life?

If we remember God's call on our lives each day when we pray, what difference might it make?

Application Question

How would you explain God's plan of salvation to a friend?

Remember that it is important to explain God's love and your response to His plan. How did it happen to you?

Close in Prayer.

Review Calendar.

Assign refreshments for next time.

During our introduction we saw how an understanding of God's grace gave way to legalism in Europe many years ago. On a sad note, the Christian Science Monitor, in an article entitled "What Place for God in Europe" published December 3, 2000 observed that this seems to have happened again. According to this article, "In 1900, Europe was home to 70 percent of the world's Christians. Today, it is home to less than 1%."

WEEK 2

RESULTS OF WITNESSING AND PAUL'S DESIRE TO VISIT ROME
ROMANS 1:8-17

Opening Prayer

Group Warm-Up Questions

Begin by considering two questions we began to think about the last time:

What word do you use to describe yourself as a follower of Jesus Christ? Believer? Christian?

Why do you say it that way? (No right or wrong answer)

Go around the group.

Remember the acronym GRACE: God's Riches at Christ's Expense, which we reviewed in our previous session. It is important to remember this concept as we work our way through the book of Romans.

Importance of Impact

It is often quite effective if we simply describe what happened to us. One's witness is inherent in this description. A wise teacher generates interest in their audience.

<u>Note</u>: One of the things that we have to combat is the pseudo-witness of some people who falsely claim allegiance to God for their own gain. Paul had it happen to him. Has anyone here run into that type of situation?

How did Paul handle it when it happened to him?

Read and comment on the following verses:

     Proverbs 16:21

     Luke 21:15

     Acts 6:10

     Colossians 4:5-6

     Ephesians 5:15-16

     James 1:5

Describing what happened to you can lead to more discussion. The words will come. The Holy Spirit will guide you. Simply explain God's love and your response to His plan of salvation. This is sometimes the most powerful witness of all.

Scripture Knowledge + Holy Spirit + Witness + Life=Powerful Result. Focus on God's Promises and a Personal Relationship with Jesus Christ.

For a number of years I had my hair cut by a woman named Karen. This sincere and intelligent woman told the whole Good News story to her clients in an interesting and enticing fashion without once reverting to religious terms. She is a positive example of making learning attractive while sharing one's faith.

Now Read Romans 1:8-17
For what was the church at Rome well-known?

What did they mean by saying "throughout the whole world?"

How did this happen in so short a time with no TV or Radio?

In this passage Paul speaks again about his commitment to God. How does he describe this commitment?

Having seen Paul's commitment to God, how would you describe his commitment to his audience?

It was really hard for Paul to get to Rome. Why did he want to get there so badly? List several answers from different people.

Read Acts 19:21 and add to the list if necessary.

Read: Romans 1:14

Colossians 3:11

Titus 3:3-4

How did Paul's attitude differ from what we see from Moses in Numbers 11:11-15?

What do we learn by observing God's use of these two very different people to accomplish His purposes?

What were Paul's unique qualifications to explain the Gospel?

Read and Explain: Acts 5:33-39

Read and Explain: Philippians 3:4-7

What was the significance of Paul's education under Gamaliel?

Paul was indeed uniquely qualified. He was quite possibly the best read, most highly educated, most intelligent man of his time. Paul Knew the scriptures that were then in existence. He had a great advantage because of his heritage and training.

Gentiles can (and must) also study and know the Old Testament. However, even after all is said and done, when a Gentile speaks of the Old Testament, it is like a blind man describing color. Believing Jews, with their heritage, training and culture bring a great richness to it.

Read Romans 1:16-17 again. This would seem to be the theme of the whole book of Romans. To whom, according to this passage, does God grant salvation?

Why does it say to the Jews first?

What is so special about the Jews? List as many things that come to mind as possible.

Having reviewed the list of the group, be sure that it includes the things below that we all need to realize are important about the Jews.

1. The Jews are God's chosen people.

2. The Jews have been the custodians of Scripture.

3. The Scriptures themselves are Jewish in nature.

4. The Jews are the people through whom the Messiah came.

5. The Messiah for all mankind is a Jewish Messiah.

6. Jesus Christ is Yeshua Ha-Mashiach (in Hebrew), the Jewish Messiah.

7. Jews and Gentiles alike both have the same problem—both still need salvation.

8. Jewish background is of great advantage in understanding the Scriptures as a whole.

Read and explain the following verses:

Romans 11:17-18

Romans 11:23-24

Mark 7:24-29

John 4:22-24

Reread Romans 1:16-17
How does a person become righteous?

What does a person's faith accomplish?

What does faith mean?

How does reliance on His Word come into play?

What kind of positive reports would you want people to hear about your faith?

How does it help someone when you remember them in prayer?

How does it help *you* when you remember them in prayer?

Why do Christians sometimes feel ashamed of the Gospel or hesitant to share?

Read Philippians 1:28. Remember and review the Concept of the *doulos,* the bond slave, what it means, and the power and authority of such an individual.

Having read these verses and reviewed this concept, does it make any sense for a believer ever to feel ashamed of the Gospel?

Now go around the group and answer this question.

For what reasons are you confident that the Gospel is true? (To paraphrase Aristotle: It works like nothing else. This comes from the Aristotlean idea that things that are pragmatic and work are valuable and true.)

Application Question

What can you do this week to help a person for whom you are concerned regarding their spiritual life, salvation, eternal destiny?

A volunteer is needed to report on *The Privileged Planet* DVD next time.

Close in Prayer.

Review Calendar

Assign refreshments for next time.

WEEK 3

GOD'S WRATH AGAINST MANKIND
ROMANS 1:18-32

Opening Prayer

Group Warm-Up Question

If God were to deliver a state of the world speech, what do you think He would say?

Wild Bill Hickok went to a town in the old west by the name of Deadwood with his friend, Charlie Utter. Charlie said this reminded him of something out of the Bible. Bill asked what part of the Bible. Charlie said "The part where God really get's mad."

Read Romans 1:18-23 with a different person reading each verse.

What is God's response to those who ignore and disobey him?

God never condemns without a just cause. Here we see three bases stated for His judgment of the pagan world: suppressing the truth, ignoring God's revelation, and perverting God's glory. Let's look at each of these a little more deeply.

1. **Suppressing the Truth.** (Read Romans 1:18)

In the New Living Translation, it says "Pushing it away from themselves."

2. **Ignoring God's Revelation.** (Read Romans 1:19-20)

Read: Exodus 10:16

> 1 Samuel 5:7-8, 11

> 1 Samuel 4:7-8

> Jonah 3:7-9

Let's hear the report on *The Privileged Planet* DVD about the Cosmos and its design.

Discuss A. E. Wildersmith and *Man's Origin, Man's Destiny*.

Discuss *Science Speaks* by Peter Stoner

Discuss *Evidence That Demands a Verdict* (several volumes) by Josh McDowell

Review/view other books and DVDs.

Read Psalm 19:1-6

Why does our society militantly insist on bad science?

What attributes of God have been clearly seen since creation? (Power and divine nature.)

What is the real issue non-believers are struggling with when they ask with belligerence, "What about the Muslims?" or "What about the Africans?"

Read: Matthew 7:7-8

        Luke 11:9-10

        Revelation 3:20

What does Jesus promise in these passages?

What excuse does man have for not knowing God?

What are two ways man needs to respond to God in light of who He is?

Read and discuss Psalm 8:1-4.

3. **Perverting God's Glory.** (Read Romans 1:21-23)

What kinds of things do people today put in place of God? (This is a bigger insult than saying there is no God.)

Review the book *God Doesn't Believe in Atheists*: *Proof That the Atheist Doesn't Exist by Roy Comfort.* As this book says and common sense tells us, there really are no atheists. Everyone has a god or gods which rule their lives.

Read Romans 1:21-32

What happens to the thinking of people who ignore and reject God? (Their ability to recognize and receive truth is impaired.)

Read and explain the following:

Ephesians 4:17

Ephesians 4:18

Romans 1:31

John 3:19-20

Matthew 13:10-16

What is a clear sign of a decadent and self-worshipping society?

What happens to people who choose this lifestyle?

Note: If such people say they have a genetic defect we can say that we do too. It is sin/rebellion and there is a solution.

Read Romans 1:25

What other deeds and attitudes result from what we see in Romans 1:25?

List these deeds and attitudes.

Instead of judging us, God has provided a remedy.

Some people like to read I Corinthians 13 substituting the words *Jesus Christ* for the word *love*.

Application Question

Who among your friends is caught in this trap of rejecting God and needs your prayers this week? (You can share if you want to. There is no need for names.)

Close in Prayer.

Review Calendar.

Assign refreshments for next time.

For some excellent information on creationism be sure to visit www.creation.com for information, publications, and DVDs superior to any in the secular world in terms of their intellectual rigor and analysis.

WEEK 4

GOD'S RIGHTEOUSNESS REVEALED AND GOD'S JUDGMENT OF SIN
ROMANS 2:1-16

Opening Prayer

Group Warm-Up Question

When each of us became a believer we had a new boss or a new teacher, so to speak. Thinking in human terms, when each of us has had a new human boss or a new teacher, what has it been important for us to know?

A number of years ago I attended the Securities Industry Institute at the Wharton Business School at the University of Pennsylvania. When I was there they had an annual essay contest. The contest was between those who were supposed to be the rising stars at the best securities firms at the best business school. The topic was the direction of the Securities Industry and the judges were supposed to be the best business teachers in the country.

The first year I wrote the best paper in my life. I spoke about the rise of financial planning and fee based relationships that put the client and the advisor on the same side of the table. In fact my comments proved to be prophetic.

I lost.

I couldn't believe it. I thought, "How could this be?" I knew what I had done was absolutely correct and that I had written a great paper.

So for year two, with the same topic, I did something different. I studied the judges. I studied, what they liked, what they didn't like, how they liked you to say things (both phrasing and terminology), what they believed, why they believed what they believed, and how they stated what they believed.

That year, I won the top award at the best business school in the country competing against the best in the nation. I won because I knew what the judges wanted.

Read Romans 1:21

What matters is the reality of God's nature. Our ideas about it don't matter. I have a friend who is a Nazarene and when he comes across a passage he doesn't like or understand about God he says, "That's not the God I worship." You know what. It doesn't matter what my friend thinks. What matters is what the One in charge thinks.

God has been gracious in giving us his word so that there is no doubt.

Today we are going to begin by talking about judgment, judging fairly, and God's judgment. We will see how this relates to us and our lives and we will also discover 7 great principles of God's judgment.

Read Romans 2:1-4

When we judge others, what do we sometimes tend to do to ourselves?

If God judges others for their sins, what does he do to us?

For what reason do you think God is kind, tolerant, and patient with us? Now read Romans 2:1 again, this time in the King James Version.

Seven Great Principles of God's Judgment

I.   GOD JUDGES ACCORDING TO THE TRUTH

Read Romans 2:5

Here we see the use of the word _sklerotes_ from the Greek which means a gradual, continual, stubborn and obstinate hardening of the heart and will. This is the root of the English word "arteriosclerosis" which refers to a gradual and continuing hardening of the physical heart and arteries.

To help us understand this let's review:

Read: Ezekiel 16: 49-50
       Luke 17: 28-30

What was the great problem or sin of Sodom?

2.   GOD JUDGES ACCORDING TO ACCUMULATED GUILT

The focus here is that God judges all people and peoples, not when he is doing it.

Read and explain the following verses: John 5:24
>   Romans 8:1

>   1 Peter 4:17

>   Romans 2:5-11

On what basis will God render his judgments?

What are the qualities of those who gain eternal life?

What characteristics do condemned people display?

Read and explain the following:
>   Psalm 62:12

>   Proverbs 24:12

>   Revelation 20:11-15

>   Luke 16:9

>   1 Corinthians 3:8

>   Ephesians 6:8

>   Ephesians 2:9

>   1 Peter 1:9

2 Corinthians 5:10

1 Peter 1:17

Revelation 22:12

3.   GOD JUDGES AND REWARDS ACCORDING TO OUR WORKS.

Read Romans 2:11-12

How can the Jews Expect to be treated by God?

How can the Gentiles expect to be treated by God?

4.   GOD JUDGES WITHOUT FAVORITISM: GOD IS FAIR AND JUDGES FAIRLY

Read Romans 2:13-14

5.   GOD JUDGES ACCORDING TO PERFORMANCE (OBEDIENCE) NOT KNOWLEDGE

Read and explain James 2:19

Also read and explain:
    Romans 6:23

    Romans 10 9-10

    Romans 11:6

Ephesians 2:8-9

Titus 3:5

Read and memorize Galatians 5:22-23. This happens naturally. It is the fruit of a changed life.

Read and memorize Romans 12:2 (Note: You may have different verses that mean more to you. Memorize what works for you.)

Now read Romans 2:14-16

What do we learn here about God's judgment and our hearts?

6. GOD JUDGES ACCORDING TO WHAT HE KNOWS IS IN OUR HEARTS

Read Romans 2:16 again.
How do you feel about this verse? *Nervous?*

Read: Jeremiah 17:9-10

      1 Corinthians 4 5

Note: My friend Larry Norman, the father of Christian rock, was responsible for tens of thousands of people coming to Jesus. He was not welcome in many churches that judged according to the way he dressed or the way he wore his hair. But God knew his heart and used him.

7. GOD JUDGES ACCORDING TO REALITY

Application Questions

Go around the group and answer these questions, as you feel comfortable.

Can you think of a time when you judged in a manner that was not pleasing to God?

What did you do (or what can you do) to rectify this?

Pray that our thoughts will be His thoughts and our minds will be conformed to His mind, that He will transform us.

Next week, we will review a passage of Scripture that has been the root of one of the most destructive heresies in the world due to arrogance, poor scholarship, and unbelief.

This is the idea that the church has replaced Israel or that Gentiles have replaced Jews in the plan of God.

Homework: Book report on *The Road to Holocaust* by Hal Lindsey.

Close in prayer.

Review Calendar.

Assign refreshments for next time.

WEEK 5

TRUE JEWS AND CIRCUMCISION OF THE HEART
ROMANS 2:17-29

Opening Prayer

Read Romans 2:17-29

This is an interesting passage because it was written about Jews. However, like many things in Scripture, the principles discussed apply to both Jews and Gentiles. This has been confusing to some people, even some well meaning people, for several reasons.

1. Poor scholarship: Some of these people are well meaning.

2. Arrogance: God warns us about this in Romans 11. It was apparently a problem in the first century AD and continues to be so today.

3. Unbelief: They may know but deny scriptural truth that they don't like.

One problem emanating from the three reasons cited above is that they also lead to some misconceptions. For example, Israel is mentioned 75 times in 73 verses in the New Testament. In each case, it refers to national Israel and not the church. In a like sense, Jews are also frequently mentioned. In each case it is clear from history, the documents themselves, and the rest of scripture that the reference was to people who were Jewish by race and not some allegorized conception of saved Gentiles.

Before we get into the part where we apply this to our lives, let's understand and quickly dispel some of the heresies some people take from this passage. They do this by taking certain verses out of the context of the whole of Scripture, or allegorizing what they don't understand or like.

Read Romans 2:17-29 with each verse being read by a different person.

If someone did not know and believe the rest of Scripture, what incorrect ideas might they have by taking parts of this passage out of context?

How would you answer them, utilizing the whole of Scripture?

Let's see what we can learn elsewhere in the Scriptures about Israel and the Jews. Please read and summarize:

Ephesians 2:12

Romans 11:13-18

Matthew 10:5-6

John 4:22

Genesis 17:7-8

Exodus 4:21-22 (Note the implications of this)

Deut. 21:17

Deuteronomy 7:6

Leviticus 26:44-45

Jeremiah 33:24-26

Genesis 12:3

Luke 1:73

Romans 11:1-2

Romans 11:18-20

Now read 2 Timothy 3:16-17.
Which particular Scriptures was he talking about? (The Tanakh)

Read Isaiah 11:11-12 as a preface to future discussions.

Important Principles to Remember

1. God chose the Jews regarding:

   - Communicating His Revelation in Scripture.
   - Bringing the Messiah into the world for all people.
   - Making them "His People" throughout history.
   - Giving them a pivotal role in history from beginning to end.

2. The Gentile Believers are grafted in.

3. Genesis promises blessings if one blesses the Jews. (Genesis 12:3)

4. "True Jews" are like true Biafrans. Many years ago, I worked for my uncle
    who is a veterinarian. He had an assistant from the African country of
    Biafra. If you visited the assistant's apartment, he had a poster on his wall
    that asked "Are you a true Biafran?" If you were a true Biafran you were
    not only from his tribe, but you also sent money back to buy food and
    guns for the tribe. You had to be a Biafran racially as well as in terms of
    your life decisions.

The same is true about being a true Jew. A True Jew, according to the Scriptures is
one who is racially a Jew and has been circumcised in their heart via a relationship
with Jesus Christ, the Jewish Messiah. Gentiles can never be True Jews any more
than I can become a black Biafran. Although I can share some spiritual things
with Jewish people, I will still not be able to have curly hair nor change my race.

5 Minute Book Report on *The Road to Holocaust* by Hal Lindsey

Also review Appendix A: How to Avoid Error.

The importance of understanding these concepts influences the understanding
of other prophecies as well. As stated in the above book on page 128, "Just who
is a true Jew or Israelite is the most critical question in resolving the controversy
between the premillennialists and the postmillenial-dominionists. If the church is
now and forever Israel, and if Christians are permanently the only true Israelites,
then the contentions of the dominionists are justified.

But, if there is still a future for national Israel, and if the Church is a distinct and
separate program of God from them, then the premillenialist position is justified.

The Holy Spirit's logic here is inescapable. He shows that God's election of Israel is the same as His election of individuals. In fact, God's dealing with Israel as a nation is a picture of how he deals with us as individuals."

With all of this in mind, let's go back and apply this to us.

Read Romans 2:17-20

How did some of the Jews think of themselves in relationship to the Gentiles?

How do they feel about this today?

Do you know of any modern day "Pharisees?" If so, can you understand how Jesus felt about them?

Read: Isaiah 29:13
        Romans 2:21-24

Of what did Paul accuse the Jews?

Read Romans 2:24
Why did they do this?

Read and explain:
        Exodus 20:7

        Deuteronomy 5:11

Discuss the "minced oaths" of some denominations. What if someone says gosh darn, holy smokes, son of a gun, that stuff---or worst of all--- Jimminy crickets?

What does it mean to take the Lord's name in vain?

Relate this to Romans 2:24, Ezekiel 36:16-24 and a consistent life.

Now read Romans 2:25-27
What was the purpose of circumcision?

What modern or scientific facts do we know about circumcision?

Circumcision acts like a surgical vaccine against a wide variety of infections, medical conditions and fatal diseases including penile and prostate cancer, thrush, urinary tract infections, and inflammatory dermatoses. It also protects the wife substantially from cervical cancer. This has always been true. God knew then and He knows now.

Read Genesis 17:12
Why did God say to do this on the 8th day?

Note: Vitamin K and prothrombin reach their maximum levels on this day to make circumcision effective. If done earlier, the baby risks hemorrhaging.

Read Romans 2:28-29
According to this, what is even more important than physical circumcision?

Read Deuteronomy 10:14-16

Application

Read Jeremiah 4:4
What are some of the ways you might be able to tell if someone has experienced this circumcision of the heart? Let's list the qualities that one might find in the lives of people who have experienced this.

God does not call us to judge other people. However, He does expect us to be "Fruit Inspectors." That is, we are to be wise enough to tell if one's life exhibits the qualities that the Scriptures tell us emanate from a circumcised heart.

Read Philippians 1:11. This is what we are to have.

Read: Romans 2:24
        Galatians 5:22-23

Pray that because of the circumcision of our hearts we will all bear the fruit of the spirit—love, joy, peace, patience, kindness, goodness, faithfulness, humility, and self-control. Pray that this will be evident in our lives to everyone and that we will then be better able to share the Word of Life from the Scriptures. Thank God for his gift of life now and eternally and the chance to share it and live it out.

Close in Prayer

Review Calendar

Assign Refreshments for next time.

WEEK 6

THE POSITION OF THE JEWS AND GOD'S FAITHFULNESS
ROMANS 3:1-8

Opening Prayer

Group Warm-up Question
This passage says something to us about truth and about those who lie. How do you determine if a person is telling the truth?

Let's take a quick look at how God regards lying and liars.
Read: 1 Timothy 1:10
       John 8:44
       Malachi 3:5
       Hosea 7:1
       Psalm 26:4
       Revelation 21:8

Read: Romans 3:1-4
According to this, what is the advantage of being a Jew? You may want to think back to Romans 2:17-29.

Let's read Romans 3: 2 in the King James Version. Doing so may help us gain a better understanding of this verse.

The word used to refer to these "divine oracles" in the Greek language is *logion*. This means more than what we may think of. It means the Jews were the recipients of divine utterances and not just custodians of Scripture. The Greek further infers that the Jews were the very recipients of God's Promises.

Read Genesis 17:6-9 and relate this to God's promises to the Jews.
Read and discuss Jeremiah 31:35-37. You may remember this one from our previous session.
Also read Ezekiel 11:12-20.

In addition to this, we should also realize that information is embedded in the text of the Scriptures from beginning to end. Many verses in the Old Testament make prophetic reference to Jesus Christ when the writers-----and indeed the readers at the time---- did not always realize exactly what was being said. For example read Genesis 1: 26.

One of the most common parts of Jewish prayers goes like this. "Hear O Israel, the Lord our God, the Lord is One." In Hebrew this reads: *Sh'ma Israel adonoi elohenu adonai echod.*

It is important to note that the use of the word *echod* is very significant. While it does mean "one" or that "the Lord is One," it is also the same word that denotes one as in a cluster of grapes. "One" in this context is, in effect, plural and points to Jesus Christ and the Holy Spirit. It is yet another allusion to the Messiah.

Read Zechariah 12:10

> Then I will pour out a spirit of grace and prayer on the family of
> David and on all the people of Jerusalem. They will look on me
> whom they have pierced and mourn for him as for an only son. They
> will grieve bitterly for him as for a firstborn son who has died.

On the surface, this is an amazing prophecy of Jesus Christ. We know that now
since we have the benefit of hindsight. However, it is actually even more significant
than it might seem at first glance.

When you look at this passage in the Hebrew, you find that part of it is actually
un-translated.

Get out the Interlinear Bible and take a look at this passage. (By the way, if you
get your own copy of the Interlinear Bible, I suggest that you get the large print
edition.)

As we do this, we should observe that Hebrew is written from right to left. It is
interesting to note that all languages from the regions to the east of Jerusalem are
also written from the right to the left. This becomes even more interesting when
we note that all languages from the regions to the west of Jerusalem are written
from the left to the right. When you put these two facts together, it appears that
the direction in which all languages in the region are written points to Jerusalem.
Is this a coincidence?

Looking at this passage in the Interlinear Bible, we need to pay particular attention
to the letters beside the word "whom." Here we find the Alef and the Tav, the first
and last letters of the Hebrew alphabet.

Read: Isaiah 44:6-7

     John 1:1-5

     Revelation 1:7-8

     Revelation 21:1-7

     Revelation 22:12-14

Now let's read Zechariah 12:10 again, inserting the un-translated letters.

> 10 "Then I will pour out a spirit of grace and prayer on the family of David and on all the people of Jerusalem. They will look on me *(The Alef and the Tav, The Alpha and the Omega, The Beginning and the End, The First and the Last.)* whom they have pierced and mourn for him as for an only son. They will grieve bitterly for him as for a firstborn son who has died."

Beginning	End
First	Last
Alpha	Omega
Alef	Tav

The inclusion of the Alef and the Tav, when understood in relationship to the rest of Scripture, makes it absolutely clear that this is a direct reference to Jesus Christ, Yeshua Ha-Mashiach, the Jewish Messiah, our Savior, and our Lord.

This should just make chills run up and down our spines as we realize even more fully the supernatural nature of what we are reading.

I have a conjecture regarding this particular passage. As we know from prophecy, in the future there will be a large group of Jews sharing the good news of Jesus Christ. My guess is that with their knowledge of the Old Testament, which they call the Tanakh, they will use this particular passage, _including the Alef and the Tav_, to great advantage.

My further guess is that when Christ returns and establishes His millennial kingdom, this hidden treasure in the text will be common knowledge.

There are many such illuminating and amazing things hidden below the surface of the text in the Bible. This is just one of thousands.

It is also important to realize that Hebrew is an alpha- numeric language. Each letter, word, and combination of letters has a numeric meaning. These alpha-numeric values, when studied, point to the Messiah and God's plan.

E. W. Bullinger, a mathematical genius, wrote a classic work on this entitled _Number in Scripture_. He lived from 1837-1913 and did all of this without the benefit of a calculator.

The back of the book reads:

> "E. W. Bullinger's classic work, _Number in Scripture_, is an invaluable guide to the study of Bible Numerics. Bullinger's two-fold approach to the subject first examines the supernatural design of the Bible. He notes the amazing patterns of numbers and numerical features of the Scriptures that give evidence of their Designer. The second section highlights the spiritual significance and symbolic connotations of the numbers which are repeated in different contexts throughout the Bible."

This is simply further incontrovertible evidence of the supernatural nature of the Scriptures that we each hold in our hands. What a privilege God has given us.

As we said when we started, this book we call the Bible is an integrated message system. Every detail is there by design. It tells us the future before it happens, while at the same time it gives us the words of life for our everyday existence.

So we see that God's Word is entirely adequate for life in a surface reading. And the deeper we go, the more we learn, even to the construction of the text.

Let's go back and read Romans 3:3-4 again.

How does failure to be true to God reflect on the character of God?

It is interesting to note that the Greek word used at the beginning of verse 4 is *genoito,* which states this even more strongly. It means "Let it not be so." Does this give you any more insight into this issue?

Let's look at a few more passages.

1 John 5:10

Psalm 51:1-4

1 John 1:9

Zechariah 12:10-13:1

Hosea 5:15

Here we see that repentance (a changing of the way) is essential to the Jew and to us as believers today.

Read Romans 3:5-8.

What was Paul's response to the charge that God is unjust in judging us?

When we realize our sinfulness, what do we learn about the character of God?

What false teaching was being attributed to Paul?

Who did Paul say deserves to be condemned and why?

What dangers result from defining our goodness in relative terms, such as comparing ourselves to Adolph Hitler, Benito Mussolini, Charles Manson, Barack Obama, your next door neighbor, the person sitting beside you, or anyone else? Let's list some of these dangers.

What excuses are we tempted to use in explaining inconsistent or sinful behavior in our lives?

How is your faith in God impacted if a supposed Christian leader is publicly found to be involved in some sinful activity? (Note: Were they really believers? The religious pseudo-Christian culture affords a safe haven for some weirdos.)

How can this not only make your faith stronger, but afford you opportunities to share your faith?

Application questions

In what practical ways can our lives be changed by the realization that God's promises will never change?

We are all aware of some of God's promises, though it is hard to keep them all in mind at once because we are limited beings. Which of God's promises do you want to keep in your thoughts this week?

Let's read one more verse that speaks about a special promise.

Read 1 John 5:11

> 11 And this is the testimony: God has given us eternal life, and this
> life is in his Son.
>
> God has given us eternal life and the power to live and enjoy a life
> that is worthwhile and honors him each and every day.

Close in Prayer.

Review Calendar.

Assign refreshments for next time.

During this session I suggest you refer directly to the *The Interlinear Hebrew Greek English Bible* as referenced in the bibliography. This experience will be further enhanced if you also utilize a copy of the Hebrew Alphabet as you view Zechariah 12: 10 in the *Interlinear Bible*.

WEEK 7

NO ONE IS RIGHTEOUS
ROMANS CHAPTER 3:9-20

Opening Prayer

Group Warm-Up Question:
If you were babysitting a two year old for one week, what conclusions would you draw about the nature of human beings? Would you say that they were perfect? Good or bad?

Read Romans 3:9-20
According to this, how are Jews and Gentiles alike?

What is the natural tendency of a human being toward God?

In what ways might you say that men and women are flawed? (Ask each gender.)

Does this apply to everyone? Even me and you?

What lessons about this topic can we draw from what we have read in prior weeks?

What about Romans 1:18-32? This says the pagan is guilty because God can be seen in creation.

What about Romans 2:1-16? This says that moral man is guilty. He doesn't even live up to his own conscience.

What about Romans 2:17-29? This says that the religious man as represented by sincere, committed, religious Jews, still doesn't make the grade.

Let's see what else the Scriptures tell us about the nature of man. Please summarize each of the following passages, focusing on what they say about the nature of man:

>   Psalm 14:1-3

>   Psalm 53:1-3

>   Psalm 5:9

>   Psalm 140:1-3

>   Psalm 10:6-7

>   Isaiah 59:7

>   Isaiah 59:8

>   Psalm 36:1

What is all of this a result of? See Romans 3:12.

These passages say a lot about our conduct and speech. Let's see what else we can learn about this from the Scriptures.

Mark 7:18-23

Matthew 12:34-37

Besides the negative statements, what positive and hopeful lesson can we learn from this passage in Matthew? (This also points to a transformed mind and heart.)

Please read and explain Romans 10:9-10.

Let's read a few more verses that give us some insight into the nature of man.

Read Genesis 6:12-13

Having read these verses the question is not "Why doesn't God save me because I am so good." It becomes "Why does God save anyone? Why does He bother?"

Now let's look at a few verses that give us some insight into what God expects from us and what He offers us.

Ephesians 6:15

Deuteronomy 5:29

How can we as mere human beings even think of doing this?

Please read and explain:

> Ephesians 3:20
>
> Philippians 2:13
>
> Ephesians 4:23-24
>
> Ephesians 4:29-30

Now that we have seen this from different angles, how would you explain Romans 3: 9-20 to someone who thinks they are good and not guilty of any serious sin?

Application Question

Are there any "laws" or "personal rules" you need to put aside in your life in favor of the true righteousness that God offers? Don't be thinking about what someone else needs to do. That's easy enough. Think about what you may need to do. (If would like to share anything about this you are welcome to. No one has to say anything.)

Pray and thank God that He has given us the gift of life and real freedom even when we did not deserve it. Let us share these gifts with the people with whom we come into contact in our world.

Close in Prayer

Review Calendar

Assign refreshments for next time.

WEEK 8

JESUS CHRIST TOOK OUR PUNISHMENT
ROMANS CHAPTER 3:21-31

Opening Prayer

Group Warm-Up Question:
Have you ever escaped a penalty you were sure you were going to have to pay? How did you feel about it?

As we read through Romans--- in fact as we read through the Scriptures--- it can be a helpful and instructive exercise if we mentally insert "The Jewish Messiah" every time immediately after we read the words Jesus, Jesus Christ, Christ, Savior, Son of God, Lamb of God, etc…Why do you think this is so?

Read Romans 3: 21-22
According to verse 21, where did this concept of a "different way" of being put right with God come from?

Read Jeremiah 23:5-6
What is the significance of the title used in verse 6?

Let's read a few more references to see where this concept originates:

> Psalm 43:1-2

> Psalm 32:1

> Isaiah 53:11

> Acts 10:43 (Where Luke helps us out in case we didn't get it yet.)

Here we see the concept of God Himself saving us.

As we move to Romans 3:22, who do we see as the source of being made right with God? (Also read this verse in the King James Version for more insight.)

How does a person obtain this righteousness?

Read: Romans 1:17

> Hebrews 11:4

> Galatians 2:16

> Romans 10:17 in the King James Version (Vitally important concept)

I have a friend who says he believes Jesus was the Son of God. He thinks this is adequate. What do you think?

To whom is the offer in verse 22 available?

Read Romans 3: 23-26
Upon Reading this, it appears in human terms that God had a problem; that is how to be just and yet justify sinful man.

Let's talk about what we might call God's greatest barrier: His own Character.

Remember what Socrates wrote to Plato in about 500 BC? "It may be that Deity can forgive sin, but I don't see how."

Let's list together some of the attributes of God's Character to help us get a better handle on this:

1. Holiness: absolute righteousness

2. Sovereign: accountable only to Himself

3. Omniscient: knows all

4. Omnipotent: All-powerful; visible and invisible

5. Omnipresent: He is everywhere (particle physics, non-locality)

6. Loving

7. Immutable: unchanging

8. Just: the standard of His character

Read: Job 25:4-6

   Colossians 2:13-14

How does providing Jesus Christ as a sacrifice demonstrate the justice of God?

Read: Hebrews 2:14-15

      1 Peter 1:18-19

Read Romans 3: 27-31
What justifies a person in God's sight?

Read: Genesis 15:6

      Ephesians 2:8

Please expound on the use of the word "believe" or "faith." What exactly does this mean?

What is the relationship between having faith and observing the law of God?

Read: Philippians 3:9
      Habakkuk 2:4
      Romans 3:30-31

Is it difficult for many people to believe that we can obtain God's forgiveness by faith in Yeshua Ha-Mashiach (The Jewish Messiah) alone? Why?

Why do some people object to the idea that God has offered forgiveness to every person, even the worst sinners?

How should what we say about our relationship with God be *different* when we realize that it is by faith alone?

What is the focus of this realization?

Let's Reread, think about, and discuss Romans 3:27.

Application Question

We each have abilities, gifts, talents, and things that we are good at. How can we communicate this to other human beings and still be certain that we give glory to God and that these things are under His control?

Close with prayer that we will exude competence and the fruit of a life changed by God in all that we do. Let us then effectively share this life with others in what we say, how we say it, and what we do.

Close in Prayer.

Review Calendar.

Assign Refreshments for next time.

WEEK 9

GOD'S SPECIAL PROMISE
ROMANS CHAPTER 4:1-25

Opening Prayer

Warm-Up Question:
What are some of the many religious acts and practices people perform in an attempt to please or gain favor with God? Just name the first one that comes to mind.

This Chapter helps us understand to an even greater degree the unity of the New and Old Testament.

As we have said, the Bible is an integrated message system comprised of 66 books written by many authors. It comes to us from outside the dimension of time, tells us the future before it happens, and has the Words of life for our everyday existence.

One of the Key Questions we want to answer today is "How was Abraham saved?"

A Personal Example of how not to discuss this

I once spoke with a person whose favorite verse was James 1:27: "Religion that is pure and undefiled before God, the Father, is this: to care for orphans and widows in their distress, and to keep oneself unstained by the world."

The out of context quote summary by which this person lived was that the true religion is to live a life of service. I asserted that, in fact, this type of religion is dead and that what is important is a personal relationship with Jesus Christ that evidences itself in a changed life.

After hearing my response to their personal rendition of Scripture, I was called a fool. My response to that evaluation of my position didn't really help the matter much. This is, perhaps, an example of how not to do it. I quoted: Matthew 5:22: "But I say unto you, That whosoever is angry with his brother without a cause shall be in danger of the judgment: and whosoever shall say to his brother, Raca, shall be in danger of the council: but whosoever shall say, Thou fool, shall be in danger of hell fire."

As I further considered our discussion for today I realized we may not all know who Abraham is. Sometimes we just assume things like this when we shouldn't.

Abraham is one of the most famous people who ever lived. Here we are, thousands of years after his death, reading and talking about him.

The generation below us does not know who Elvis Presley is.

Elvis Presley was inducted into the Contemporary Christian Music Hall of Fame recently. What other one time famous musician was inducted at the same time? (Clue: He was known as the Father of Christian Rock and Roll.)

How many here know who George Patton was? Do people 25 years old or younger know?

How about Thomas Jefferson's wife? She was famous at the time. What was her name? She was Martha Wayles Skelton, whom he married when he was 23 years old. She was already a widow at the time.

By and large people have forgotten these famous personages of the past few hundred years. But Abraham is more famous than all of them. He is better known than the most famous world leader the most famous actor, or the most famous Rock star.

Read Genesis 11:27 though Genesis 12:9

What do we learn from this? Please enumerate.

Read Genesis 17:1-8

What do we learn from this passage? Add to the list we just started.

This is even more astounding than we might realize when we understand the background from which God called Abraham.

Read Joshua 24: 2

God called Abraham out of Ur. The spiritual ruler of Ur was the moon god, named Al-ilah. Sometimes this was also spelled Al-Ilahi. Perhaps it is easier to visualize as Al-ilahi. The name of the moon god was later contracted into Allah.

Read: Romans 4:1-5

Also read: Genesis 15:6
           Galatians: 3:6
           James 2:23

What was the main characteristic of Abraham's faith relationship with God?

How might we say that Abraham was declared righteous before God?

What were the three main components of Abraham's faith relationship with God?

1.   Intellectual Assent.

2.   Actual Trust.

3.   Action.

Was Abraham also declared righteous because he did most everything right?

Who can remind us of a couple of really big mistakes that Abraham made? (Read Genesis 12:10-20 and Genesis 20:1-17 if we have time. If we don't have time, perhaps someone can give us a quick summary.)

Read Romans 4: 6-8

Read Psalm 32:1-2

How did David feel about this process of being made right with God? Why was this such a big deal to him?

Read Romans 4:9-12

Read Genesis: 17:9-10

What was the relationship between Abraham's righteousness and his circumcision?

What was the purpose of circumcision in Abraham's life?

Was there an additional purpose below the surface on a medical basis?

On what basis can both the circumcised and the uncircumcised claim Abraham as their father?

Note: This still does not change Gentiles into Jews on a racial basis.

Read: Genesis: 17:15-17

     Genesis 18:1-15

     Genesis 17: 5

     Hebrews 11:11

     Hebrews 11:12

If time permits, read Genesis 22:1-18 and comment on the process of faith continuing to play out in the life of Abraham.

Read Romans 4:13-19

On what basis did Abraham receive God's promise about inheriting the world?

Read Romans 4:20-22

How was Abraham able to resist the temptation to doubt God's promise?

Read Luke 1: 37

Read Romans 4:23-25

Let's also Read 1 Corinthians 15:1-4.

Some people without a clear understanding of the scriptures claim that this is contradicted by James 2:14-24.

Read James 2:14-24

How does this passage coincide with and further explain what we read in Romans 4 and elsewhere in the scriptures today?

Application Question

How does God's relationship with Abraham help you understand His workings in your life?

Close in Prayer.

Review Calendar.

Assign refreshments for next time.

WEEK 10

FAITH, PEACE, JOY, ENDURANCE, HOPE, ENEMIES, JUSTIFICATION
ROMANS 5:1-11

Opening Prayer

Group Warm-Up Question

What results can difficult circumstances have in a person's life?

Read Romans Chapter 5:1-11
Read Romans 5:1 again.

In your own words, how would you describe the concept spoken of here as justification?

The word "with" in this verse is *pros* in the Greek and incorporates the meanings: "face to face, intimate relationship, and understanding."

How does this greater understanding of the language affect our understanding of this verse?

This verse speaks of peace. Let's try to understand just exactly what God is saying to us by relating it to other scriptures.

Read: Isaiah 32:17

      Ephesians 2:14

      Colossians 1:20

      John 14:27

      John 16:33

      Philippians 4:6-7

Let's summarize now and list the various characteristics of this peace with God.

Is the believer responsible for having peace in the sense of making it, or having peace in the sense of claiming and enjoying it?

Read John 14:27 and John 16:33 again.

Read Romans 5:2.

I understand that the Greek word for access used here is "*prosagoge*" and means "privilege of approach" and insinuates something that has happened in the past with results that continue on; nothing changes it.

How does this meaning of "privilege of approach" affect your understanding of this verse?

Let's look at a few more scriptures to give us a fuller understanding of this privilege we have, why we have it, and what it means.

John 10:9

John 14:6

Ephesians 2:18

Romans 11:6

Colossians 2:6

Colossians 3:4

2 Thessalonians 2:14

How can we summarize what we learn from these verses?

Now let's move on and read Romans 5:3-5 one verse at a time.

As I understand it, the Greek word for "troubles" or "tribulation" used here is *thlipsis*, which means "a pressing, pressing together, affliction, distress, dire straits, or distress that is brought about by difficult circumstances."

We also see that the Greek word for "knowing" is "*eido*" which means "perceive, notice, discern, discover."

How does this understanding affect our reading of Romans 5:3? If helpful, reread the verse inserting these definitions.

Let's now read a few other verses that help us to have a greater grasp of these vitally important concepts.

> Matthew 5:11-12
>
> Acts 5:41
>
> 2 Corinthians 12:10
>
> James: 1:2-3
>
> 1 Peter 3:14
>
> James 1:12

How can we summarize our understanding of these verses.

Now let's take a look at: James 1:2.

How is it possible for us to do this?

Read: Romans 5:5 again.

> 2 Corinthians 6:1-10
>
> Ephesians 4:30
>
> 2 Corinthians 1:21-22
>
> Ephesians 1:13-14
>
> 1 John 3:24
>
> 1 John 4:13

As we think upon all of this, what good things can result from suffering?

As we go through life we must always remember what we learn in Romans 8: 28. Please read this verse.

Read Romans 5:6-11

What was our relationship to God when Christ came to die for us?

If God has demonstrated His love for us through Jesus's death, what can we anticipate concerning our future relationship with God?

For what reasons, then, can a believer rejoice?

What kinds of things, thoughts, and attitudes can keep us from being full of joy and hope in the middle of difficult circumstances?

How can suffering produce positive rather than negative results?

Read Romans 8:28 again.

Application Question

In what difficult circumstances do you need to stop grumbling and stay focused on the joy of life in Christ?"

Close in prayer.

Review calendar.

Assign refreshments for next time.

WEEK 11

DEATH THROUGH OUR RELATIONSHIP WITH ADAM, LIFE THROUGH OUR RELATIONSHIP WITH CHRIST
ROMANS 5:12-21

Opening Prayer

Warm-Up Question:

In what ways can the decisions of a few leaders impact the lives of millions and how do you feel about it?

Read Romans 5:12-14

This particular passage and concept has been a source of discomfort to many and, at the same time a great blessing. It has been a source of discomfort because many people are not happy with the choice Adam made as their representative, and the effect it has on all people and them in particular. Conversely, it has been a great blessing because of the redemptive and life giving action of Jesus Christ and the universal availability of life through Him.

How did the giving of God's law affect the presence of sin in the world?

Let's take a further look at how this happened and what it means.

Read: Genesis 2:1-25

Genesis 3:1-25

Having read these verses, what do you see as the root cause of death?

What exactly does the scripture mean here when it speaks of death?

Read: Galatians 3:10

James 2:10

Read: Romans: 5: 15-17

How are Adam and Christ Similar and at the same time different?

	Similar	Different

Read: Romans 6:23

> Philippians 3:9
>
> 1 Corinthians 15:21-22
>
> 1 Corinthians 15:45
>
> Isaiah 53:11
>
> Matthew 20:28
>
> Matthew 26:28
>
> Isaiah 1:18
>
> Luke 7:47

What, specifically, came into the world through Jesus Christ?

How can we best explain the impact of the promise in Romans 5:17?

Read and discuss John 10:10.

Read Romans 5:18-21

What effect did (and does) God's righteous law have on rebellious people?

List these things.

What does sin in this world produce?

What does grace given by God produce?

List the things produced by the grace that God gives.

Read: John 1:16-17

Titus 2:11

Hebrews 4:16

1 Peter 5:10

Application Questions

How can knowing you are forgiven and righteous before God, through Jesus Christ, affect your attitudes and actions?

What can you do this week for friends still suffering from the consequences of sin?

Close in prayer.

Review calendar.

Assign refreshments for next time.

WEEK 12

DEAD TO SIN, ALIVE IN CHRIST
ROMANS 6:1-14

Opening Prayer

Group Warm-Up Question:
What motivates people to make major changes in their lives?

Read Romans 6:1-14
Why should a person who has been set free by Christ try to live a good life and not sin?

Does this have something to do with a vow we have made or with what God has done? Explain.

Read: Romans 2:4

Romans 3:8

1 Peter 2:24

What do you think of when you hear the word "baptism?"

We see the word "baptism" mentioned in Romans 6:3-4. This word has a wide latitude of meanings and is seen in both the New and Old Testament. There are many different types of baptism mentioned in the Bible. In fact, there are at least 7 different kinds. In most references we see the concept of "identification with" somehow associated with Baptism. Let's take a look at a few references to help us get a handle on this:

    1 Corinthians 10:1-2

    1 Peter 3:20-21

    Acts 18:24-28

How do these verses relate to the concept of baptism?

How did John's Baptism differ from the Baptism of Jesus?

Read: Acts 19:1-5

    1 Peter 3:21

    Galatians 3:22-27

    Matthew 3:11

    1 Corinthians 12:12-14.

    Acts 1:5

    Acts 11:1-18

Some have said that I Corinthians 12:13 defines "Baptism of the Holy Spirit." How do you feel about this?

We generally view baptism as a one-time event.

Every believer has been "baptized" by the Holy Spirit." However, the ongoing filling of the Holy Spirit must be claimed every day. How do you feel about this statement?

What makes it possible for a person who has become a believer to live a new life?

Read Romans 6:4 again.

How does this relate this to our discussion?

Some denominations and people get caught up in using religious words, jargon, or supposedly spiritual terms. One of the terms being thrown around in some circles is that of "sanctification," or alternatively "entire sanctification." While this is a term found in Scripture, it is sometimes confusing when not clearly identifying the ongoing process to which it refers.

Read Romans 6:5-11 for some important insight to this process.

How does God help a person discard old habits and tendencies?

Read and discuss Ephesians 4:23-24, which gives us further insight into exactly what is happening through this process.

Read: Philippians 2:13

     Philippians 3:12-14

     Philippians 4:8

     1 Thessalonians 5:16-20

Application Question

How can you actively resist the temptation to sin and at the same time effectively offer yourself as an instrument of God during the coming week? Be as specific as you wish. Feel free to cite any specific circumstance or situation that you are facing.

Homework: 5 Minute Book report on *Be Ye Transformed* by Nancy and Chuck Missler for next time.

Close in prayer.

Review calendar.

Assign refreshments for next time.

WEEK 13

FREEDOM, SLAVERY, AND OBEDIENCE
ROMANS 6:15-23

Opening Prayer

Group Warm-Up Question:
What bad habits can control and damage a person's life?

Read Romans 6:15-18
Who or what determines the things that dominate a person?

Read: Matthew 6:24

Luke 16:13

Why shouldn't a believer continue to disobey God (to sin) willingly?

Read: John 8:34

> 1 Peter 2:17-22
>
> Romans 13:12
>
> 2 Corinthians 6:7
>
> 2 Corinthians 10:4-5 (Be sure to give us your perspective on exactly what this verse refers to.)
>
> Philippians 2:12-13

What attitude should believers have as they obey their new master?

Read Romans 6:17 in several versions. How does it apply to the above question?

Read: 2 Timothy 1:13

> Colossians 2:6

Read Romans 6:19-23

What is the result of being a slave to sin or disobedience?

Note: In verse 23 the Greek word that we read as "wages" originally meant "a soldier's pay," something to which he was entitled in return for what he had done.

How does your understanding of the underlying Greek in this passage affect your understanding of this concept?

Read: Romans 1:32

    Proverbs 1:31

    Proverbs 14:12

    James 1:15

    Luke 16:24-25

What is the result of receiving the gift of God referred to in Romans 6:23?

Read: Ephesians 2:8-9

    John 8:32

    John 8:36

    1 Corinthians 7:22

    John 10:10

What results of this Freedom should we see in our lives?
Read Galatians 5:22-23

What long-term benefit do we receive as a result of God's gift to us?

Read: John 4:14

    John 10:28

5 Minute Book report on *Be Ye Transformed* by Nancy and Chuck Missler

Application Question

In what areas of your life do you need God's help to resist the temptation to act in a way not pleasing to Him?

Close in prayer.

Review Calendar.

Assign refreshments for next time.

GOD'S PERFECT LAW AND OUR
RELATIONSHIP TO IT
ROMANS 7:1-6

Opening Prayer

Group Warm-Up Question:
In our world there are many generally accepted myths about human nature, education, responsibility, accountability, human development, crime, and our actions. Let's go around the group circle and see how many generally accepted myths of our culture we can enumerate. (Be sure we touch upon how one gets to heaven, Darwinism, crime and our environment, man's state of "constant" improvement, education, etc.) (As an example, our friend Marilyn feels certain that all of the problems experienced by radical Muslims would disappear if they were only to be educated.)

List as many generally accepted myths of our culture as possible.

Read Jeremiah 17: 9

Note that in Jeremiah 17:9 the word used for "desperately" in Hebrew is *anash*. This insinuates weakness, sickness, frailness and that man is incurably wicked. This is one of the most important and often reluctantly accepted doctrines of serious Bible students.

Are the myths of our time based upon either scripture or verifiable truth?

Why do you think we see these myths operating and existing in our world?

Read Romans 7:1-3

Do you think God is telling us this again to only reiterate things about marriage or is He also getting at something else?

Read: Romans 7:4-6

What exactly is Paul talking about when he refers to the law?

How many commandments are there in the Tanakh?

Read Exodus 20:1-17

Which commandment is different than all the others and how is it different? (17)

Some people say they live by the Ten Commandments. Some say they live by the Sermon on the Mount. Let's look at the Sermon on the Mount for a moment.

Read Matthew 5:1-48

Portions of this passage are very often taken out of context and misquoted or purposely misapplied.

What one or two words apply to anyone's claim that they truly live by the commandments in the Tanakh or the Sermon on the Mount?

What does the husband represent in Romans 7:1-3?

What does the wife represent in this same passage?

In Romans 7:4-6 it again refers back to "fruit." To what is this referring?

Reread (or recite from memory) Galatians 5:22-23 (Special Congratulations to anyone who is able to recite this without looking it up.)

Let's take a few moments and contrast the letter of the law to the spirit of the law spoken of in Romans 7:6. Read Romans 7:6 again.

Now let's look up a few verses. After reading each verse please comment upon how this relates to living by the letter of the law or the Spirit.

	Letter	**Spirit**
Dependent Upon:	Romans 8:3	Acts 1:8
Produces:	Romans 7:8	Philippians 2:13

Results in:	Romans 5:20	Romans 8:4
Brings:	Galatians 3:10 Romans 4:15	Galatians 5:22-23
Regarding Faith:	Galatians 3:12	Galatians 5:5 2 Corinthians 5:7

Read: Philippians 2:13

     Galatians 3:21

     2 Corinthians 3:4-6

What role, then, does God's law play in a Believer's life?

What problems can one encounter by a strict adherence to even a well-intentioned set of rules developed by men to ensure adherence to God's law?

Application Question

What can you do this week to build your living relationship with Christ, instead of merely following the rules?

Close in prayer.

Review calendar.

Assign refreshments for next time.

WEEK 15

CONFLICT, DISCOURAGEMENT, AND VICTORY
ROMANS CHAPTER 7:7-25

Opening Prayer

Group Warm-Up Question:
How do you tend to respond to authority?

Read Romans 7: 7-13
What is the purpose of the law?

What bad effect does knowing the law have on a person?

How do children respond when they see a sign that says "Keep off of the Grass?" Why?

What was the effect of prohibition in the United States of America? Why?

How does knowing the law bring the possibility of death to a person?

Read Romans 7:9 again.

What does this imply about small children?

Read 2 Samuel 12:15-23

How does this dovetail with Romans 7:9, and what does it tell us? (Note: These verses are viewed as the basis for children being saved prior to the age of accountability.)

Are people still guilty without the law?

Read and discuss Romans 1:18-20.

Read Romans 7:14-25

What did Paul share about his own attempts to follow the law?

What are some of the various ways people respond to God's law?

To understand the problem both we and Paul have here, let's slowly read through Romans 7:14-22 and carefully note each time we see such words as "I, me, mine, my, etc..."

What insight might this give us into our situation?

How can a believer continue to commit sins even though they have given their life to God?

What is the solution to this dilemma?

Read and discuss:

    Romans 7:24-25

    1 John 3:6-9

    Romans 5:17

What should we do if we become discouraged and confused in our Christian lives?

Read and discuss:

    Philippians 3:12

    Hebrews 10:24-25

    Psalm 119:133

    Ephesians 4:22-24

    Romans 8:1-2

    Romans 8:5-11

How can knowing that God has achieved the ultimate victory over sin affect our prayers, attitudes, and thoughts?

Application Question

How can you remind yourself each day this week of God's victory over sin?

Close in prayer.

Review calendar.

Assign refreshments for next time.

WEEK 16

LIFE THROUGH THE SPIRIT
ROMANS 8:1-17

Opening Prayer

Group Warm-Up Question:

If you were released from a three-year captivity as a hostage, what would you do during your first week of freedom?

The 8th chapter of Romans is perhaps the most inexhaustible chapter in the Bible.

Read Romans 8:1-4

What is the status of a person who trusts in Jesus Christ?

How is a person set free from the law of sin and death?

Read: John 3:14-16

   John 5:24

   Galatians 5:21

Read Romans 8: 5-8

What is the difference between those who live according to their sinful nature and those who live according to the spirit?

Read and discuss Galatians 5:22-23. This is a helpful passage to memorize.

Romans 8:6 speaks of death. Let's discuss various kinds of "death" that we find in the scriptures.

1.   Physical Death: When the soul leaves the body. Matthew 8:22

2.   Spiritual Death: Ephesians 2:1

3.   Reproductive Death: Romans 4:19

4.   Positional Death: Romans 6:3-5; Colossians 2:3-4

5.   Operational Death: Ephesians 5:14-18; Revelation 3:1; Hebrews 6:1; Hebrews 9:14

6.   Second Death: Revelation 20 6; Revelation 20:14

Read Romans 8:9-14

How can a person know if he or she is controlled by the sinful nature or the Spirit?

What promise is given to people living in the spirit?

What kind of obligation do believers have?

Read Romans 8:15-17

In Roman law, adoption was required, even of a legitimate son if he was to inherit. This ceremony, legally held in the Forum, was called the "Adoption." All born in a man's family were children. Only those adopted were recognized as sons. After adoption they could never be disowned.

What insight does the Roman concept of adoption, with which Paul's audience was familiar, give you into these verses?

In the most literal sense, the word *Abba* in Hebrew means "Leader of the House" and coveys a deep sense of endearment, love, or intimacy. Many people today liken it to "Daddy."

Even people who have never had a real "Daddy," or who have had an abusive father, can find such a daddy-type of relationship with the Creator of the universe when they become believers. This is an unfathomable privilege.

Read Romans 8:15 and Mark 14:36

What is the significance of this double usage of the word "Abba?"

What does unchecked sin and selfishness do in a person's life?

What have you seen the spirit of God do in a person's life?

Application Question

What changes have you been resisting in your life that you are now willing to allow your loving heavenly Father to complete? (If you're not comfortable sharing something personal, just share your thoughts on the process in general.)

Close in prayer

Review calendar

Assign refreshments for next time.

WEEK 17

THE ROLE AND USE OF TRIALS, SUFFERING, AND OUR HOPE
ROMANS 8:18-27

Opening Prayer

Group Warm-Up Question:

Go around the circle. What types of sacrifices are people often willing to make in order to obtain a future reward?

Read Romans 8:18-27

How did Paul describe the difference between his present circumstances and his future?

Read John 16:33

What kinds of suffering did Paul endure during his lifetime on earth? Please enumerate.

Read: 2 Corinthians 11:21-28

2 Corinthians 4:7-18

How would you characterize Paul's overall view of trials and suffering?

What are some of the Reasons that Believers Experience Suffering?

Daniel 3:1-29 (To Glorify God.)

Hebrews 12:5-11 (Discipline and growth)

1 Peter 4:1-2 (Keep from falling and, at the same time, equipping.)

2 Corinthians 12:7-10

1 Peter 1:6-7 (Build faith.)

Romans 5:3-5

Philippians 4:11-13

2 Corinthians 1:3-4

2 Corinthians 4:7-11

What examples of this have you seen in everyday life?

Read: James 1:2-4

Romans 8:19

How do you relate Romans 8:19 to what you see in the world today?

In what other specific ways do you see this happening or not happening today?

For what, specifically, are the children of God waiting?

Read: Romans 8:22-25

2 Peter 3:10-13

What is the nature of genuine hope?

Important note: The use of the word "hope" in the Greek is the opposite of our use of the word in English. In the Greek, "hope" is a confidence, sureness and knowledge of future things. In fact, in the Greek, the word "hope" infers a certainty stronger than knowing. It is an ultimate, internal, overpowering, all-enveloping, eternal surety and truth that is absolute.

It has been said that those people with the greatest hope show the greatest stability under stress. How do you feel about this statement?

Read: 2 Corinthians 4:16-18

How does the Holy Spirit help us in our weakness?

Read: Romans 8:26-27

Who else is pleading for us?

Read: Romans 8:35

　　　Hebrews 7:24-25

　　　Hebrews 11:32-40

How do these verses speak to us about the interrelated nature of hope and faith?

Read: 1 Corinthians 10: 13

Application Question

In what circumstances of your life do you fully need to realize the patience, confidence, and hope spoken of in 1 Corinthians 10: 13?

Close in prayer.

Review calendar.

Assign refreshments for next time.

WEEK 18

OVERWHELMING VICTORY AND ETERNAL SECURITY
ROMANS CHAPTER 8:27-39

Opening Prayer

Group Warm-Up Question:
How can you explain why "bad" things happen to "nice" people?

Before we delve into this passage itself, let's revisit the concept of Inheritance from our session on the first part of Chapter 8. There we reviewed the Roman concept of adoption. In Roman law, adoption was required even of a legitimate son if he was to inherit. This ceremony, legally held in the Forum, was called the "Adoption." All born in a man's family were children. Only those adopted were recognized as sons. After adoption, they could never be disowned.

In Contrast to this we also see in the Old and New Testament the concept of an inheritance, or reward, received for a life of faithfulness. This type of inheritance can apparently be forfeited even though the status of being adopted as a child of God does not change.

Read Luke 15:11-32

What insight does this passage give you into the biblical concepts of Adoption, inheritance, and rewards?

How did Jesus achieve his inheritance?

To help us understand, read Philippians 2:7-11.

What was the effect of this achievement?

To help us understand read Hebrews 2:10.

What caused Esau to lose his inheritance?

To help us understand read Hebrews 12:16-17.

How can one be sure of their inheritance?

To help us understand read Hebrews 6:10-12.

Read Romans 8:27-39

To whom is the promise in Romans 8:28 made?

What are the 3 most important words in this verse?

Note: The active voice of the Greek verb *synergei* ("He works together") emphasizes that this is a continuing activity of God.

Under what condition is it possible for a person to lose their salvation? (Answer: If it is based on their own works and worthiness.)

If someone asks if it is possible to lose their salvation, you can say that it is possible for them to lose theirs if it is based upon their own efforts. (This means they never had it.) However, it is not possible to lose ours since it is based upon the sacrifice of Christ and the promises of God.

The Foundation and Basis of Our Eternal Security

1.   GOD'S SOVEREIGN PURPOSE.

Read: Ephesians 1:11-14

     Hebrews 6:17-20

2.   GOD'S SOLEMN PROMISE.

Read: Romans 4:16

     Genesis 15:6

     Romans 4:23-24

     John 3:16

3.   His Infinite Power.

Read: John 5:24

   John 6:39

   John 10:27-29

4.   His Unfathomable Love.

Read: Romans 5:6-10

   Romans 11:29

   Romans 8:32

   Romans 8:38-39

5.   God's Answer to the Prayer of His Son.

Read: John 11:41-42

   John 17

Read: Romans 8:29-30

It has been stated that uncertainty about God's election arises from some kind of self-righteousness. How do you feel about this?

This can be a difficult concept, especially for those who limit God to their self-imposed human abilities. In the Scriptures, we have a God who calls us, who gives us a choice, and who knows the beginning from the end. Only our all- powerful and all-knowing God is capable of such things. (Regarding the opportunity for salvation, which is available to all, you may find it helpful to read Acts 2:21, Romans 1:16, Romans 10:13, 2 Peter 3:15 and 1 Timothy 2:2-4.)

Seven Important Questions About Our Eternal Security

1.   CAN OPPOSITION DEFEAT THE BELIEVER?

Read: 1 Peter 5:8

     Romans 8:31

     Ephesians 6:11-13

2.   WILL WE HAVE THE RESOURCES WE NEED TO PREVAIL?

Read: Romans 8:32

     2 Peter 1:3

     Romans 5:6-10

3.   WILL OUR HUMAN FRAILTIES AND FAILURES REVERSE OUR BEING MADE RIGHT WITH GOD?

Read: Romans 8:33

     Romans 3:24

     Romans 5:1

     Romans 8:1

4.   Can Anyone Condemn Us For Any Reason?

Read: Romans 8: 34

     Romans 8: 1

5.   Can anything separate us from His love?

Read: Romans 8:35-39

6.   What kind of assurances do we have of victory?

Read: Romans 8:38-39

     Revelation 17:14

7.   How does this happen on a day-to-day basis in the life of a believer?

Read: 2 Corinthians 5:17

     Galatians 5:22-23

Application Question

How can you commit your difficult circumstances to God this week?

Note: A suggested memory verse for each of us is Romans 8: 28.

Close in prayer.

Review calendar.

Assign refreshments for next week.

WEEK 19

ISRAEL IN THE PAST
ROMANS 9:1-29

Opening Prayer

Group Warm-Up Question:

How do you react when someone claims that God is on their side?

Romans 9-11 gives us Paul's definitive statement on Israel:

Chapter 9: Israel in the past.

Chapter 10: Israel in current times.

Chapter 11: Israel in the time to come.

These same verses also give us many lessons for our day-to-day living that we cannot ignore. It is our goal to see both what the Scripture has to say about Israel while also learning what these passages have to say about our lives today.

Read: Romans 9:1-29
What was Paul feeling when he wrote this passage?

Read: Psalm 119:136

      Luke 19:41

Read: Romans 9:1-5
What special gifts, privileges, and opportunities did God provide to the Jews? Please list as many as possible.

Read: Deuteronomy 7:6

      Acts 3:25

      Deuteronomy 26:18-19

      Deuteronomy 10:15

Read: Romans 9:6-9
What did Paul mean when he said that everyone born into a Jewish family is not truly a Jew?

What is a true Jew?

Can a Gentile become a true Jew?

Discuss true Biafrans.

Read: Romans 2:28-29 for a reminder.

    Galatians 4:28

Read Romans 9:10-15
How did Paul respond to the accusation that God is unjust in choosing the Jews or certain people for certain things?

Read Deuteronomy 32:4.

Read Romans 9:16-18
What determines how God bestows favor on people?

Read Exodus 9:16.

Read Romans 9:19-24
Why does God show patience with us even though we deserve His wrath?

Read: Daniel 4:35

    Isaiah 45:9

    2 Timothy 2:20

    Ephesians 4:7

Read Romans 9:25-29

What do we learn from Hosea about the Gentiles?

What do we learn from Isaiah about the Jews?

What implications does Paul's burden for Israel have on our lives today?

On what basis does God choose people to inherit His promises?
Read Ephesians 2:8-9

Application Question

When can you take time this week to thank God for His acts of mercy and love to you?

Assign for Next Time: 5 Minute book report on *As America Has Done* by John McTernan

Close in prayer.

Review calendar.

Assign refreshments for next time.

WEEK 20

GOD ALWAYS KEEPS HIS PROMISES
(ROMANS 9: 30 THROUGH
ROMANS 9:30-ROMANS 10:21
PART I

Opening Prayer

Group Warm-Up Question:

Do you really enjoy reading the book of Numbers? Why or why not?

Romans 9-11 gives us Paul's definitive statement on Israel. In addition, these same verses give us many lessons for our day to day living that we cannot ignore. It is our goal to see both what the Scripture has to say about Israel while also learning what these passages have to say about our lives today.

One of the overriding messages that we want to remember from this material is that God always keeps his promises.

Many churches, while giving lip service to the Scriptures, twist and turn and hedge and allegorize when they are uncomfortable with the concept that God says what He means and means what He says.

We want to be sure to study diligently to learn what He says to us through His integrated message system. We must remember that this comes to us from outside the continuum of time. Every detail is there by design. This includes every place name, every word, every letter, every verb tense, every punctuation mark, even to the order of the words. Rabbis who are serious about the Scriptures say that the Messiah will even explain the meaning of the spacing between the words to us.

The Covenants

In God's Word we find a number of vitally important covenants for us to understand.

Four Unconditional and Unilateral Covenants Essential for Understanding God's Word

1. **The Abrahamic Covenant**. This is found in Genesis 12:2-3, where God makes seven very important "I will" statements.

Read: Genesis 12:2-3

> And I will make of thee a great nation, and I will bless thee, and make thy name great; and thou shalt be a blessing:
>
> And I will bless them that bless thee, and curse him that curseth thee: and in thee shall all families of the earth be blessed.

Let's list together the 7 "I will" statements made by God in this passage.

1.

2.

3.

4.

5.

6.

7.

Are these "I will" statements unilateral or bilateral?

What actions have the Jewish People or the Nation of Israel needed to take to lay claim to these statements?

How does this covenant relate to God's plan for all mankind?

Read: John 4:22
     Genesis 17:3-4
     Genesis 17:7
     Genesis 17:13
     Genesis 17:19

Note: All other covenants build on this one.

Listen to the Book Report on *As America Has Done* by John McTernan.

2. **The Palestinian Covenant**. Please read Genesis 12:7 and Genesis 13:12-18.

For Later Reading:

You may want to see the sealing of this Covenant in Genesis 15:9-21.

You can see the passing on of the title to this land to Israel: Genesis 35:9-12.

You can learn about the prophesized Dispersion of Israel in Deuteronomy 28:63-68.

Leviticus 26:40-45 and Deuteronomy 30:1-3 shed more light on this.

For many years, the Jews were scattered among the nations. What did this lead some people to conclude about:

The promises of God?

The object of the Palestinean Covenant?

The Position or elevation of the Gentile Church?

Why do you think this happened?

Read: 2 John1:9

Jude 1:4

Revelation 3:9

What happens if we stray away from Scripture and interject our own agendas?

To understand what happened to Israel in regard to the land read Ezekiel 36:17-32. Why did God bring Israel back to the land given them?

3. **The Davidic Covenant**. Please read: 1 Chronicles 17:11-14.

To whom do you believe I Chronicles 17:11-14 was referring?

For Later Reading:

    2 Samuel 7:11-16

    Psalm 89:3-4

    Psalm 89:33-34

    Psalm 132:11

    Genesis 49:10

    Isaiah 9:6-7

Having made these promises, God "lost patience" with the royal family of David. He seemed to invalidate His promise when Jehoiachin was cut off.

Read Isaiah 7:13

13 Then Isaiah said, "Listen well, you royal family of David! You aren't satisfied to exhaust my patience. You exhaust the patience of God as well!

Read Jeremiah 22:30

30 This is what the Lord says: Let the record show that this man Jehoiachin was childless, for none of his children will ever sit on the throne of David to rule in Judah. His life will amount to nothing."

Satan and his minions must have been laughing with delight at what they thought was the failure of God's covenant. This seemed to mean that God made a cosmic mistake and that the Messiah could no longer come as promised. However, God was more than one step ahead.

To understand this, let's look at the genealogies of Jesus as presented in the New Testament documents.

The Two Genealogies

As a Levite, Matthew focuses on the Messiahship of Jesus and traces the legal line from Abraham through David, then Solomon and the royal line to Joseph, the legal father of Jesus. This is how any Jew would do it. (Matthew 1:1-17)

When we read 2 Samuel 5:14, along with Matthew 1:1-17, we see that Joseph was also of the line of David as traced through David's son, Solomon.

In Luke 3:23-38, Luke focuses on the humanity of Jesus and also traces the blood line through David. Then he veers off and traces it through Nathan, a different son of David, to Mary, the mother of Jesus.

Mary was of the line of David, but through Nathan, not Solomon.

See 1 Chronicles 14:4

4 These are the names of David's sons who were born in Jerusalem: Shimea, Shobab, Nathan, Solomon,

Later read Genesis 17:2-8

As we already discovered, the Jews traced their genealogy through the father's bloodline. In this case that would be Joseph. However, under the blood curse, the line through Joseph would not work.

How can the Messiah be of the royal line and yet not be subject to the blood curse? This seems somewhat impossible.

How do you get a descendant of David if the descendant is traced by blood through the father when the curse prevents that from happening?

God's loophole, for the benefit of the attorneys in our group.

One must note the amendment to the law which permitted inheritance through the daughter if no sons were available and she married within the tribe.

Read 1 Chronicles 7:15

15 Makir found wives for Huppim and Shuppim. Makir's sister was named Maacah. One of his descendants was Zelophehad, who had only daughters.

Read Numbers 27:1-11 One verse at a time.

1. One day a petition was presented by the daughters of Zelophehad—Mahlah, Noah, Hoglah, Milcah, and Tirzah. Their father, Zelophehad, was the son of Hepher, son of Gilead, son of Makir, son of Manasseh, son of Joseph.

2. These women went and stood before Moses, Eleazar the priest, the tribal leaders, and the entire community at the entrance of the Tabernacle.

3. "Our father died in the wilderness without leaving any sons," they said. "But he was not among Korah's followers, who rebelled against the Lord. He died because of his own sin.

4. Why should the name of our father disappear just because he had no sons? Give us property along with the rest of our relatives."

5. So Moses brought their case before the Lord.

6. And the Lord replied to Moses,

7. "The daughters of Zelophehad are right. You must give them an inheritance of land along with their father's relatives. Assign them the property that would have been given to their father.

8. Moreover announce this to the people of Israel: 'If a man dies and has no sons, then give his inheritance to his daughters.

9. And if he has no daughters, turn his inheritance over to his brothers.

10. If he has no brothers, give his inheritance to his father's brothers.

11. But if his father has no brothers, pass on his inheritance to the nearest relative in his clan. The Israelites must observe this as a general legal requirement, just as the Lord commanded Moses.' "

Later read:

Numbers 26:33

Numbers 36:2-12

Joshua 17:3-6

Here we see how the inheritance can be passed through Mary.

But now we have a bigger problem.

Although the inheritance can thereby pass through the mother, how do you do so without involving the blood curse from the blood line of the father, Joseph?

Mary seems to have made this all the more difficult by marrying someone from the bloodline of Solomon.

Mary can pass on the inheritance, but the inheritance can have nothing to do with the physical bloodline of the father, Joseph.

Did Mary marry the wrong guy?

Read: Isaiah 7:14

    Luke 1:30-33

Note: God solved what seemed an insurmountable problem so far as human knowledge and experience goes.

Christ's Geneology as the pre-existent One

Read: John 1:1-3

Looking forward we also find The New Covenant with Israel, which is not to be confused with what is generally referred to as the New Covenant or the New Testament. (See Hanukkah, the blood sacrifice and atonement, and the fulfillment in Jesus Christ)

Read Jeremiah 31:31-34

Note: While this refers to Israel at a future point in time, many people would also say that these things should be evident in the body of believers right now.

For more information, later read Ezekiel 37:21-28

Application Question

Today we saw God's hand in these irrevocable covenants and in history. How will this impact your relationship with God this coming week?

Close in prayer.

Review calendar.

Assign refreshments for next time.

WEEK 21

GOD ALWAYS KEEPS HIS PROMISES
ROMANS 9:30-ROMANS 10:21
PART II

Opening Prayer

As we said in Part I of this portion of our material, Romans 9-11 gives us a Paul's definitive statement on Israel. In addition, these same verses give us many lessons for our day to day living that we cannot ignore. It is our goal to see both what the Scripture has to say about Israel while also learning what these passages have to say about our lives today.

One of the overriding messages that we want to remember from this material is that God always keeps His Promises.

Many churches, while giving lip service to the Scriptures, twist and turn and hedge and allegorize when they are uncomfortable with the concept that God says what He means and means what He Says.

We want to be sure to study diligently to learn what He says to us through His integrated message system. We must remember that this comes to us from outside the continuum of time. Every detail is there by design. This includes every place name, every word, every letter, every verb tense, every punctuation mark, even to the order of the words. Rabbis who are serious about the Scriptures say that the Messiah will even explain the meaning of the spacing between the words to us.

Group Warm-Up Question: How carefully do you follow the instructions in a ready-to-assemble product?

Read Romans 9:30-33

What big problem were the Jews having that was preventing them from getting right with God?

Do you think this was a "surprise" to God?

Read: Psalm 118:22

    Isaiah 8:14

    Matthew 21:42

    1 Peter 2:6

Why do you think this was (and still is) such a problem for the Jews?

Read: Leviticus 17:11

    Hebrews 10:1-4

    Hebrews 9:27-28

Is this same "Stone" also a stumbling block for Gentiles today?

Read 1 Corinthians 1:23

Why do you think this is so?

Read Matthew 5:17-20

Read Romans 10:1-4

What is the relationship between Christ and the law in a person's pursuit of righteousness?

Galatians 3:17-26

Read Romans 10:5-15

Why is it important to "Believe in your heart and confess with your mouth" as noted in Romans 10:10?

What great promise do we have in Romans 10:11?

Read Matthew 10:32-33

Read Romans 10:16-21

How legitimate are the claims of people who claim ignorance of Jesus as savior?

Is this country a Christian or pagan nation?

How can a person have great zeal for God or religious activities and be misguided?

Application Question

Who in your family or circle of friends needs to hear about God's plan for putting people right with himself? When do they need to hear?

Close in Prayer

Review calendar

Assign refreshments for next time.

WEEK 22

GOD'S MERCY AND THE REMNANT OF ISRAEL
ROMANS 11:1-10

Opening Prayer

Warm-Up Question:

How would you turn down an invitation to a vitally important event that your boss wanted you to attend?

Read Acts 17:11

Remember that Scripture is our guide and authority as we discuss these sometimes difficult topics.

Read Romans 11:1-6

How did God answer Elijah's call to destroy Israel?

How did Paul answer those who believed that God had rejected the Jews?

What caused the remnant of Israel to survive?

What characteristic separated the Jews who had not turned away in Elijah's time from those who had?

Read 1 Corinthians 4:7

What has God chosen by grace?

Why did God bother saving a remnant of the Jews throughout history when they had been so disobedient?

Read Genesis 12:2-3

Note: While this most definitely is oriented toward Israel and the Jews, we should also realize that the destiny of the entire world hangs on these promises.

What causes God's people to turn away from Him?

What causes people raised in believing families, churches, or communities to turn away from Him?

Read Romans 11:7-10

Who are those spoken of in Romans 11:7?

What does it mean in Romans 11:7-8 that some were "made unresponsive?"

We need to engage in a careful reading of the text here and in the rest of scripture to try to understand this.

Read Romans 11:8 again.

Specifically, what happened to those that were unresponsive?

How did this happen? Paul gives us some important clues in Romans 11:9-11.

Why did these people turn away from God?

Read Romans 9:31

The Greek text in Romans 11 seems to indicate that these people were judicially given over to the hardness of their own hearts. How does this help our understanding of this passage?

Does a hardened heart absolve one of personal responsibility for their actions anywhere in Scripture?

Answer: NO. You can't blame God for your hardened heart.

What hardens a person's heart against God?

In the context of all of this discuss the concept of the Life Mile or Parade. This concept incorporates two ideas. The first is that we all have a "life mile to run." We don't know how long this mile or our lives will be, but our lives have a beginning and an end on this earth. The second part of this concept is that while we do not know when our lives will end or what will happen, God has a different perspective. In a sense, He sees our lives as one might see a parade from a helicopter hovering above the procession. Time is a construct by which we measure our lives. God exists outside of the construct of time as we know and experience it. This is a difficult idea for many people to accept. The concept of free will is as vital to the Scriptures as is the concept of God's foreknowledge. These ideas are actually complementary when one understands the nature of God as revealed in the Scriptures.

Discuss the following verses; specifically, why is God telling us these things? What do they mean to us and the world at large?

John 10:27-28

John 6:35

Mark 10:15

James 1:25

1 Peter 1:10

Revelation 3:19-20

1 John 2:3-6

1 Peter 4:11

2 Peter 3:9

Colossians 3:23-24

Revelation 17:14

Application Questions

What can you do this week to avoid the influences that harden a person's heart toward God?

What can you do this week to encourage a Believer who feels outnumbered or overwhelmed?

Close in Prayer

Review calendar.

Assign refreshments for next time.

WEEK 23

GRAFTED IN
ROMANS 11:11-24

Opening Prayer

Group Warm-Up Question:

What success have you had in gardening? Is it easy or does it take some work?

Read Romans 11:11-16

What hope do the Jews have of ever recovering their relationship with God?

What is the significance of the fact that the Jews have stumbled but not fallen?

What effect did the Jews rejection of Jesus have upon the Gentiles?

According to Romans 11:12, what greater result is coming from all of this?

How does Romans say this will happen?

Is this a new idea?

Read Deuteronomy 32:21

How could this kind of thing possibly lead someone to a relationship with Christ?

Read Romans 11:17-24

How would you summarize the illustration that Paul uses to describe the situation of the Jews and Gentiles?

What warning does God give to the Gentiles in this passage?

Why is this so important?

What is promised to Jews who do not persist in unbelief?

Why have some Gentiles been tempted to feel superior to Jews?

What attitude should we have toward the fact the God has chosen to reach out to us?

Now, this may all seem quite clear to us at this point. However, we must also realize that replacement theology is not only alive and well, but it is one of the most prevalent and destructive heresies in the world today. (You might recall that replacement theology assumes that the church has replaced Israel in the plan of God and therefore the promises made to Israel devolve upon the church.)

Let's think together about some of the destructive results of the unscriptural position that is adopted in replacement theology and list them below.

Why do you think so many people in the world at large and in the institutional church find their Heretical adherence to replacement theology to be so attractive? List these reasons.

Over the coming years you will come into contact with people who have bought into this unscriptural teaching. Let's take a look at a few references and see what they tell us about the situation of such people as well as how we should conduct ourselves.

2 John 1:9

Jude 1:4

1 John 2:3-6

2 Peter 3:16-17

Hebrews 4:12

James 1:25

Note: One of the Lies that always seems to always accompany replacement theology is the assertion that the Israelis today have displaced the modern-day nation of Palestine, (which in fact never existed).

In addition, those who promulgate replacement theology also engage in continual non-sequiturs and twist the scriptures. I have included some additional scriptural references in Appendix B (Still Chosen, with Additional Scripture References) that may be helpful to you when you encounter such situations.

Application Question

What can you do this week to acknowledge that you depend on God's kindness and the truth of His Word?

Close in Prayer

Review calendar.

Assign refreshments for next time.

WEEK 24

ALL ISRAEL WILL BE SAVED, GOD KEEPS HIS PROMISES
ROMANS 11:25-32

Opening Prayer

Group Warm-Up Question:

What would it take to get you knowingly to break an important promise that you made?

Interesting Quote from Sir Isaac Newton (A.D. 1643-1727)

Sir Isaac Newton was an English physicist, mathematician, astronomer, natural philosopher, chemist, and theologian who is considered by many scholars to be one of the most influential people in human history. He is most remembered for his classic works on the laws of gravitation and the physics of motion. He developed the first reflecting telescope and shares credit with Gottfriend Liebniz for the development of differential and integral calculus.

To sum it all up, he was a pretty smart guy, who also, most importantly, was a believer.

This particular quote is interesting to read as we enter into today's study:

"About the time of the End, a body of men will be raised up who will turn their attention to the prophecies, and insist upon their literal interpretation in the midst of much clamor and opposition."

Read Romans 11:25-27

To what mystery was Paul referring in these verses?

Where does this idea come from?

Read: Deuteronomy 4 25-31

       Deuteronomy 30:1-6

       Hosea 14:1-7

       Joel 2:12-3:2

What does all of this show us about God's promises?

The Greek word used in Romans 11: 25 for "hardening" is *porosis*. This seems to indicate a blindness or hardness such as the covering of a callous; obtuseness of mental discernment or dulled perception; the mind of one which has been blunted; of stubbornness or obduracy.

What do you see as the significance of this?

Read Romans 11:28-32

When does it seem that this will all happen?

Read: Matthew 23:37-39

     Luke 21:24

     Romans 11:25 (again)

     Jeremiah 30:14

     Jeremiah 30 in its entirety (For later reading)

     Joel 30 (For later reading)

     Zechariah 12:10

     Zechariah 13:1

     Zechariah 12 (For later reading)

     Psalm 2 (For later reading)

Note: The Greek word for "fullness of the Gentiles" is *pleroma*. This is a maritime term for a ship that is fully manned with sailors, rowers, soldiers, etc...

What insights do these references as well as the Greek explanation, give you?

We should note that Bible scholars with a strong foundation in the Old Testament agree that in order to understand what time it is on God's prophetic time clock we need to view things through the lens of Israel.

Where in history do you think we are now?

Read 1 Corinthians 13:8-12

How does our commitment to God affect his dependability and trustworthiness?

Read Deuteronomy 7:8

For some who take verses out of context, Romans 11:26 has been confusing. They use it as an excuse to not share God's truth with Jews. To be sure we are clear on this, let's answer the questions they ask:

Does this passage mean that every single Jew will be reconciled to God?

Is this speaking corporately about Israel?

What must an individual Jew do to be saved?

How does this relate to both Jews and Gentiles?

For Help in putting this all together:

Read: Romans 9:27

     Romans 11:5

     Romans: 11:26

Joel 2:32

John 14:6

Romans 11:32

What response should we have to all of this?

Read: Matthew 24:14

Matthew 28:19-20

2 Peter 3:9

Application Question

Which of God's promises do you need to focus on and memorize this week?

Close in prayer.

Review calendar.

Assign refreshments for next time.

For more information, please refer to Appendix C: Mathematical Prophecy of the Return of Israel.

WEEK 25

GOD'S RICHES, POWER,
WONDER AND WISDOM
ROMANS 11:33-36

Opening Prayer

Group Warm-Up Question:

What was your idea of God when you were a child?

Read Romans 11:33-36

How did Paul describe God's judgments?

Read Romans 11:33 again, this time in the King James Version.

The Greek word here that is translated "unsearchable" is *anexereunetos*. Interestingly, this literally means "incapable of being traced by footprints."

135

How does understanding the literal meaning of this word in Greek impact your understanding of Romans 11:33?

This same word, *anexereunetos,* is used one other place in the New Testament. Read Ephesians 3:8

When we view these two verses together, how does this impact our understanding and comprehension?

Read Romans 11:33-34 again.

How did Paul describe the mind of God?

Read: Isaiah 40:13-14

      Job 41:11

What force or power is higher or wiser than God?

What about the President of the United States of America?

What about those human beings you answer to?

What about the IRS?

Read Romans 11:35 again.

What does God owe us?

Read: Job15: 8

Jeremiah 23:18

What does God need from us?

Read Job 35:7

What do you make of this verse?

Why, then, should we be "good" as defined in the Hebrew Scriptures?

Read Romans 11:36 again.

What is God's place in the universe?

Read: John 1:3

Colossians 1:16

Revelation 4:11

Read Romans 11:33-36 again.

Why does Paul praise God?

Read: 1 Corinthians 1:31

    Romans 16:27

    Revelation 5:12-13

Many people in our world, even believers, sometimes doubt God. When one understands the facts, the magnitude and the authority of God's Word, this becomes an untenable position. We should all be aware that the Bible is the world's greatest and only infallible authority on all facets of human knowledge. This includes economics, science, psychology and everything else.

Here are a few examples of what some call "Hidden Treasures" in the Biblical text.

Read Job 26:7 to see how the earth exists in space.

Read Hebrews 11:3 to learn about the atoms and molecules.

Read Genesis 6:15 to learn about the perfect dimensions for a stable water vessel.

Read Deuteronomy 23:12-13 and Leviticus 15:13 to learn about sanitation.

Read Job 38:16 to learn about springs in the ocean.

Read Psalm 4:7 to learn about human emotions.

Read Genesis 1:20-22 to solve the chicken and egg dilemma.

Read Isaiah 40:22 to learn that the earth is a sphere.

Read Romans 1:20-32 to learn that rejecting the Creator results in moral depravity.

Read Genesis 7 and 2 Peter 3:5-6 to learn about the flood that resulted in world-wide fossil evidence and the future irrational denial of this event later on.

Read Genesis 1:9-10 to learn about one central land mass giving way to the "continental drift."

Read Jeremiah 1:5 and Exodus 21:22-23 to learn that life begins at fertilization and that killing an unborn child is considered by God to be murder.

Read Psalm 19:6 to see that the sun travels in a circuit, 3000 years before humans figured it out.

Read Job 38:35 in the King James Version to learn about radio and light waves and the use of them to transmit speech.

Read Proverbs 17:22 and 18:14 to learn that laughter promotes healing and that a negative attitude has harmful physical effects.

Read Leviticus 23:22 and 25:1-24 to learn about effective organic pest control and land management.

What effect should our knowing all of these things have on our everyday lives?

Read: Psalms: 119:75

     Romans 8:28

     1 Peter 4:11

Application Question

What is at least one specific way you can reflect God's character to others through your life?

Close in prayer.

Review calendar.

Assign refreshments for next time.

Note: The wisdom, brilliance and riches of the creator are available for anyone with an open mind to observe. To see this put in terms of "modern science," I suggest you access some of the excellent resources available from Creation Research at creationresearch.net. This team of eminently competent and honest scientists, led by John Mackay, clearly shows how a correct application of the scientific method verifies the scriptural record. Of course, whether or not "modern scientists" realize the truth of the Scriptures, the Scriptures themselves are nevertheless absolutely reliable. If current science is too primitive to understand eternal truths then it is our scientific methodology which needs to be improved in order to be honest and effective. The eternal Truth in the Judeo-Christian Scriptures remains forever, regardless of the good or bad opinions and methodology of men.

WEEK 26

A LIVING SACRIFICE
ROMANS 12:1-8

Opening Prayer

Group Warm-Up Question:

Besides your relationship to Christ, what things or experiences have significantly shaped your perceptions, thought processes, and emotions?

Read Romans 12:1

Please read Romans 12:1 in at least two versions, being sure that one of them is the King James Version.

To what does the word "therefore" refer?

According to this, how can one most properly worship God?

In this verse we also read about God's mercies. The Greek word used for "mercies" is *oiktirmos.* In a literal sense, this may be understood as compassion. This word also appears elsewhere in the New Testament.

Take a look at the following verses to see some of the places this word appears to see how the usage of *oiktirmos* there impacts our understanding of Romans 12:1. For this exercise the King James Version may be helpful, augmented by other translations.

Read: 2 Corinthians 1:3

      Philippians 2:1-4

      Colossians 3:12

      Hebrews 10:28

Romans 12:1 also speaks of sacrifice.

How do you see this sacrifice as being different from the Old Testament sacrifice for sin?

Read: Romans 6:13

      Romans 6:16

      Romans 6:19

How do you see this bodily sacrifice playing itself out in actual practice in day-to-day life?

Read: 1 Thessalonians 5:23-24

    Hebrews 13:15-16

As a result of this bodily sacrifice, what vitally important position do believers have in the world?

Read: 1 Peter 2:5

    1 Peter 2:9

    Revelation 1:6

Read Romans 12:2

How should the mind of a believer be different from that of an unbelieving person?

How does this process take place?

What are some of the benefits of this process that we see enumerated in this verse?

Note: The Greek word used here for "transformed" is *metamorphousthe*. We recognize this as the source of the English word metamorphosis. It infers a total change from the inside out. And, like the metamorphosis of a caterpillar to a beautiful butterfly, is also means "keep on being transformed."

Note: See the book *Be Ye Transformed* by Nancy Missler, which we discussed earlier in this series.

How does our understanding of the Greek text impact our understanding of Romans 12:2?

For further insight, let's read Ephesians 4:22-24.

In a very practical sense, how do we access the ability to do this in our lives on a daily basis?

Read Ephesians 6:10-18 for an excellent summary of this process.

Note: Many believers have found it helpful to read and pray through these verses as with other passages of scripture.

Read Romans 12: 3-5

How should a believer think of him or herself?

Read: Proverbs 11:2

   Proverbs 16:18

   Proverbs 6:16-19

What heads the list in the passage from Proverbs 6?

We have read here about the importance of making an honest appraisal of oneself. Some call this humility. It is also said that a person's self-esteem is immeasurably raised by the love of God. How can we reconcile these two seemingly contradictory thoughts?

Read Proverbs 29:23

Read Romans 12: 6-8

What specific gifts does Paul enumerate in these verses?

Which believers have spiritual gifts from God?

Read Galatians 4:7

Which gift is the best?

How are we to apply these gifts?

If time permits, read:

> 1 Corinthians 12:12-27

> Ephesians 4:15-16

Application Question

What spiritual gift or gifts from God can you see in your life, and how can you put a spiritual gift to work to benefit others this week?

Close in prayer.

Review calendar.

Assign refreshments for next time.

WEEK 27

SOME OBSERVABLE EVIDENCES OF A SPIRIT FILLED PERSON
ROMANS 12:9-21

Opening Prayer

Group Warm-Up Question:

What might a friend do to you that you would have trouble forgiving?

Discuss the repentance/forgiveness cycle. This means that, in terms of the biblical concept of forgiveness, forgiveness is complete only when there has been a true changing of one's way. Without it, the cycle is not complete, effective, or pleasing to God. It is, in effect, a sham without repentance. Many sociopaths and other bad actors have done some dastardly things and then tried to say to the world, "but God forgives." True students of the Scriptures know that for the plan of God to be complete, the circle must be completed by repentance and a renewed heart and mind accompanied by the work of the Holy Spirit in one's life. This cycle, when in action, can be readily observed by most anyone.

Read Romans 12:9-21
Many people think that our faith is only about love. Here we are actually told to hate in a qualified sense. What are we told to hate?

How are we to define what to love or hate?

Read: 2 Timothy 3:16-17

      1 John 2:27

What specific instructions about love do we find in Romans 12 verses 9-10? List these instructions.

Read Romans 12:11 again.

Why is this concept so important?

Read Ephesians 6:5-8

In Romans 12:12 we are admonished to do three important things. How would you put these three things in your own words?

Read Romans 12:13

What were the best know motel chains at the time this was written? (Motel 6? Holiday Inn? Ramada? Marriott?)

Note: In the East today, especially in the absence of places to stay for travelers, hospitality is regarded as a sacred duty.

In Paul's day "hospitality" meant putting up travelers, without charge, in one's home while they were in town. The travelers would normally carry letters of introduction from people trusted by their hosts, attesting that they were to be accepted as guests. Neither they, nor we, were told to take the concept of welcoming strangers into our homes mindlessly out of context to the detriment of all involved.

Revisit Romans 12:13

How do you think believers in the first century would have responded if they saw modern believers living in luxury while other believers in the same city were living in poverty?

How should we respond?

Read 2 Thessalonians 3:8-10

Read Romans 12:14

Read Matthew 5:44-47

Do you think Paul was remembering his personal situation as recorded in Acts 7:59-60 when he wrote Romans 12:14?

Read Romans 12:15

Read 1 Corinthians 12:26

What effect does it have when believers do this?

Read Romans 12:16-21

Read: 1 Thessalonians 5:15

     1 Peter 3:8-9

     Proverbs 25:21-22

How are we to respond to our enemies?

What is the result of this response?

What is the importance of the second half of Romans 12:18? Why do you think God included this qualifier?

How does this dovetail with our responsibility as delineated in Matthew 5:13?

Application Question

Whom do you need to love or bless this week even though they may be part of the enemies camp?

Close in prayer.

Review calendar.

Assign refreshments for next time.

Special Assignment: Read and report on the book, *The Sacred Rights of Conscience; the Selected Readings on Religious Liberty and Church-State Relations in the American Founding* by David Dreisbach and Mark David Hall.

WEEK 28

A BELIEVER'S CALL TO ACTION
ROMANS 13:1-7

Opening Prayer

Group Warm-Up Question:
How do you feel when you have to prepare your income taxes?

Introduction

This chapter is one of great importance. It also contains verses that have been taken out of the context of the whole of Scripture and misused to the detriment of our faith, to the detriment of communities, and the detriment of nations on a larger scale.

Our goal is to see this passage in light of the whole of Scripture and not in view of any particular bent anyone may have toward pacifism, fatalism, activism, rebellion, capital punishment or politics.

We would do well to read and remember the following verses:

> 2 Timothy 3:16-17

> Acts 17:11

Some of the questions people have wrestled with over the years as they relate to the specific verses in Romans 13:1-7 have been:

Must we obey a government that is corrupt?

How do we, as believers, relate to a government that is a representative republic? (This is a relatively new phenomenon in human history.)

Do we, perhaps, have dual citizenship?

As we first open our Bibles to Genesis 1-11 we find that God has ordained a number of vital concepts and institutions. These include:

FREE WILL

The framers of the American Constitution, most of who were believers, had a profound understanding of this. We should also understand that free will is a prerequisite for love.

MARRIAGE.

God provides a model for intimacy.

The Family

This institution has immeasurable responsibility in a society for teaching respect, authority, relationships, godliness, etc. The state cannot successfully replace the family and create a healthy society with healthy people.

Human Governance

Read Romans 13:1-7

What presupposition of Paul's is endemic to our understanding of these verses?

What standard of conduct in relationship to the established laws of society should a believer follow?

Read: Acts 4:18-21

  Matthew 11:1-2

  Matthew 14:3-4

What are some of the key attributes of a good or bad leader?

Read: Proverbs 16: 2

  Proverbs 20:28

  Proverbs 29:4

  Proverbs 29:12

  Proverbs 31:4-5

In a country with a representative government, what are our responsibilities as "employer voters?"

What very general characteristics should we be looking for in the people we support for public office in a representative government?

Read: Proverbs 8:12-15

        Romans 2:14-15

Specific Requisite Activities of the Believer Toward Government

1.   PRAY FOR OUR PRESIDENT

If applicable, pray for the president's repentance. Pray for faith, honesty, and purity of heart, body and mind. Pray for the moral leadership of the office to be pleasing to God.

2.   PRAY FOR ALL OF OUR LEADERS

Pray for wisdom, courage, and repentance when applicable.

3.   ACTIVELY SUPPORT CANDIDATES OF PROFOUND PERSONAL INTEGRITY

4.   HOLD ALL ELECTED OFFICIALS ACCOUNTABLE

5.   COMMUNICATE WITH THOSE IN GOVERNMENT ABOUT YOUR VIEWS.

The other side is already doing this. Note the tremendous negative effect of the CAIR and other groups on the 2010 National Day of Prayer. (You can find the e-mail addresses for your elected officials at www.house.gov and www.senate.gov.)

Book Report on Recommended Reading: *The Sacred Rights of Conscience; the Selected Readings on Religious Liberty and Church-State Relations in the American Founding* by David Dreisbach and Mark David Hall.

Some forensic historians claim that to understand the intent of the framers of the U.S. constitution, one must read Romans 13:1-7 with the knowledge that they understood the authorities in a representative republic to be themselves.

What does this say to us about our responsibilities today?

Remember (and Perhaps Memorize) 2 Chronicles 7: 14

> 14 If my people, which are called by my name, shall humble themselves, and pray, and seek my face, and turn from their wicked ways; then will I hear from heaven, and will forgive their sin, and will heal their land.

Read Jeremiah 12:17 and relate it to 2 Chronicles 7:14 and our very serious responsibilities. If time permits, consider also reading:

> Deuteronomy 16:20
>
> Proverbs 31:8-9
>
> Isaiah 1:17
>
> Jeremiah 4:2
>
> Jeremiah 21:12

Hosea 12:6

Amos 5:15

Amos 5:24

Zephaniah 2:3

Matthew 5:6

Hebrews 11:33-34

Read Romans 13:4-5 again.

How do these two verses relate to those who are employed in the field of law enforcement?

Which of the general principals about our relationship to the government at large are the most important in relationship to those involved in law enforcement?

Read Romans 13:6-7 again.

What important admonitions do we find here?

What negative consequences for our lives and witness can occur if we do not heed these admonitions?

Application Questions

What can you do to bring about truth, justice, and righteousness in your sphere of influence this week?

Which government official could you write or talk with this week to express your appreciation or concerns?

Close in prayer.

Review calendar.

Assign refreshments for next week.

WEEK 29

PERSONAL CONDUCT THAT PLEASES GOD AND BENEFITS EVERYONE
ROMANS 13:8-14

Opening Prayer

Group Warm-Up Question:
What sort of actions on the part of other people communicate love (not romantic love) to you?

Read Romans 13 8-10
What do you think it means when it says "Pay all of your debts?"

In which area of life is a believer to maintain a debt?

Exactly what does it mean to maintain this debt of love?

Read: Galatians 5:14

     1 Timothy 1:5

     Leviticus 19:18

     Mark 12:30-31

     James 2:8

How does 1 John 1:9 relate to Romans 13:9?

Read: 1 Timothy 1:6-14

     Matthew 22: 7-40

How is a believer's duty or debt of love converted into a delight?

Read: Galatians 5:13

     Galatians 5:22-23

God also follows up on these excellent verses with a warning in Galatians 6:3. Please read and explain this important verse.

God also gives us yet another special and wonderful promise as we experience the trials of being human and a victorious life.

Please read and explain 1 Corinthians 10:13.

Read Romans 13:11-14

What kinds of behaviors do we see enumerated that should have no part in the

life of a believer?

Now let's look at a few more verses that give us even more insight into these issues
of personal conduct. Let's enumerate the kinds of behaviors we see that should
have no part in the life of a believer.

Note: A few of these will be evident by noting the converse of a quality mentioned
in these verses. The others are pointedly direct.

Read: 1 Corinthians 15:34

      Ephesians 5:1-20

      1 Thessalonians 5:2-5

Does God really take our actions in this life seriously? After all, aren't we simply
"human?"

Read: Revelation 21:8

      1 Corinthians 6:9-10

      1 Corinthians 5:7-10

Now we come to the most important part of our investigation today.

Ingredients in the Process of Victory

By what process are we to focus on things that please God in terms of our thoughts, words and actions?

Begin a list. Read Colossians 3:9-17 and enumerate ingredients in the process of victory.

Read 1 Corinthians 10:13 and continue enumerating ingredients in the process of victory.

Read Ephesians 6:6-18 and list even more ingredients in the process of victory.

Read Ephesians 4:23-24, continue our list, and note the specific process by which this is all happening.

Read Philippians 4:8 and continue our list as we see some of what God wants us to do on a daily and continual basis.

Read 1 Corinthians 16:13-14 and finish our list for this session.

Application Question

As you embrace the victorious life from God, what specific thing can you do this week to demonstrate His love or kindness toward a believer? Toward a non-believer?

Close in prayer

Review calendar

Assign refreshments for next time

WEEK 30

NURTURING GROWTH IN
THE BODY OF CHRIST
ROMANS 14:1-15:13

Opening Prayer

Group Warm-Up Question:

What do you do when a homeless person asks you for money, and why?

Read Romans 14:1-6

What types of issues did Paul say are not worth fighting over?

Why do you think he said this?

In verses 5-6, what important aspect of a believer's belief about these types of things should be evident and in place?

Is it adequate to do what you feel is "right in your heart?"

Let's spend a little time on verses 5 and 6, since this may seem more relevant to us than what may initially seem to be surface issues of eating and drinking.

Here we come to the issue of the Sabbath.

The first mention of the Hebrew verb *shabbath*, which means "rest from labor" or "the day of rest" is in Exodus 16:23 in relationship to the gathering of Manna. Read Exodus 16:23.

> 23 He replied, "The Lord has appointed tomorrow as a day of rest, a holy Sabbath to the Lord. On this day we will rest from our normal daily tasks. So bake or boil as much as you want today, and set aside what is left for tomorrow."

We see God commanding the Israelites to observe the Sabbath in Exodus and Deuteronomy.

Read Exodus 20:8-11

> 8 "Remember to observe the Sabbath day by keeping it holy.
> 9 Six days a week are set apart for your daily duties and regular work,
> 10 but the seventh day is a day of rest dedicated to the Lord your God. On that day no one in your household may do any kind of work. This includes you, your sons and daughters, your male and female servants, your livestock, and any foreigners living among you.
> 11 For in six days the Lord made the heavens, the earth, the sea, and everything in them; then he rested on the seventh day. That is why the Lord blessed the Sabbath day and set it apart as holy.

Also review Deuteronomy 5:12-15 for a reiteration of this passage.

We also see that God declared a Holy day of rest even before this time. Read Genesis 2:2-3.

> 2 On the seventh day, having finished his task, God rested from all his work.
>
> 3 And God blessed the seventh day and declared it holy, because it was the day when he rested from his work of creation.

It was the custom of Jesus to attend the synagogue on the Sabbath. (Luke 4:16; Mark 1:21; 3:1; Luke 13:10)

The concept of the Sabbath was perverted by the Pharisees and other legalistic Jewish leaders. This perversion continues today. For example, the elevators in religious Jewish areas are set up so that you cannot even push a button on the Sabbath. They operate automatically on that day.

Read Matthew 12:10-13

> 10 where he noticed a man with a deformed hand. The Pharisees asked Jesus, "Is it legal to work by healing on the Sabbath day?" (They were, of course, hoping he would say yes, so they could bring charges against him.)
>
> 11 And he answered, "If you had one sheep, and it fell into a well on the Sabbath, wouldn't you get to work and pull it out? Of course you would.
>
> 12 And how much more valuable is a person than a sheep! Yes, it is right to do good on the Sabbath."
>
> 13 Then he said to the man, "Reach out your hand." The man reached out his hand, and it became normal, just like the other one.

Read Luke 13:10-17

> 10 One Sabbath day as Jesus was teaching in a synagogue,
>
> 11 he saw a woman who had been crippled by an evil spirit. She had been bent double for eighteen years and was unable to stand up straight.

12 When Jesus saw her, he called her over and said, "Woman, you are healed of your sickness!"

13 Then he touched her, and instantly she could stand straight. How she praised and thanked God!

14 But the leader in charge of the synagogue was indignant that Jesus had healed her on the Sabbath day. "There are six days of the week for working," he said to the crowd. "Come on those days to be healed, not on the Sabbath."

15 But the Lord replied, "You hypocrite! You work on the Sabbath day! Don't you untie your ox or your donkey from their stalls on the Sabbath and lead them out for water?

16 Wasn't it necessary for me, even on the Sabbath day, to free this dear woman from the bondage in which Satan has held her for eighteen years?"

17 This shamed his enemies. And all the people rejoiced at the wonderful things he did.

Note: Jesus is recorded as healing on the Sabbath 7 times. This number is likely significant.

Does anyone have any ideas on why this may be significant?

Jesus emphasized the purpose of the Sabbath.

Read Mark 2:27

27 Then he said to them, "The Sabbath was made to benefit people, and not people to benefit the Sabbath."

What are the physiological, psychological and spiritual results of observing or not observing a weekly day of rest?

Interestingly, the evidence is that the early church leaders did not consider Sunday as a continuation of the Hebrew Sabbath. Saturday was, and still is, observed by the Jews as the Sabbath. Some Gentile believers also have become enamored of this practice.

Most Gentile believers and many Jewish believers now effectively treat Sunday as the day of worship and rest. We are exhorted to continue the practice of meeting and worshipping together. This is a necessary part of a healthy faith.

Read Hebrews 10:25

> 25 And let us not neglect our meeting together, as some people do, but encourage and warn each other, especially now that the day of his coming back again is drawing near.

Regular meetings and worship are assumed throughout the New Testament. (See John 10:19; 2 John 1:10; James 2: 2; Philemon 2; Colossians 4:15; 1 Corinthians 16:19; 1 Corinthians 14:23-35; 1 Corinthians 11:17-18, 34; Romans 16:23; Romans 16:5; Acts 15:7; Acts 5:12; Acts 4:31; and Acts 2:1 among others.)

Many scholars also take Isaiah 66:22-23 to mean that the Sabbath will continue in the millennium.

Now, let's reread Romans 14 5-6 and sum up this particular issue.

Read Romans 14:6-8 again.

What are to be the most important aspects of the choices we make in regard to these issues, and indeed, to all of our choices in life?

Read Romans 14:9-13

Why does this judgment of others sometimes become a problem?

To whom must we and other believers all answer?

Knowing this, how should we behave toward other believers in regard to these issues?

Read Romans 14:14-16

What makes our choices about these types of issues wrong or right?

Read Romans 14:17-22

What should our attitude be as we approach non-essential issues?

Read Romans 14:23 –Romans 15:3

Should we actually encourage those who have a different idea than we do about non-essentials, even though we disagree with them about these things?

So far, Paul has mostly spoken directly of food and drink. These are pretty easy issues for us today in most situations. However, if we carefully examine these verses we can see that he is also talking about other non-essential and potentially divisive areas of thought, belief, and action. What other areas of life might also fall into this same category?

What should guide our individual thoughts, beliefs, and actions in regard to all of these things?

Read: 2 Timothy 3:16-17 (We should all know these verses by heart.)

    Galatians 5: 22-23

Note: We frequently go back to these verses since these concepts are so vitally important.

Read Romans 15:4-13

Why were these issues regarding our personal opinions dealt with in the Scriptures long ago?

According to verse 7, what is the ultimate template for our relationship with other believers?

If this is the template, upon what basis should one become dictatorial, belligerent, or hostile about their personal non-essential opinions as they relate to other believers?

Read Romans 15:9-11 again.

Also read Psalm 117

What other activity should we be engaging in as we put this all together?

Read Romans 15:5-6, 13 again.

What is to be the ultimate result of maintaining proper relationships with other believers?

Application Question

What can you do this week to spread positive mutual acceptance, understanding, and edification among believers?

Close in prayer.

Review calendar.

Assign refreshments for next time.

WEEK 31

A TRUE JEW TAKES THE MESSAGE OF LIFE TO THE GENTILES
ROMANS 15:14-22

Opening Prayer

Group Warm-Up Question:

What foreign culture interests you the most, and why?

In *The Wiersbe Bible Commentary: The Complete New Testament in One Volume*, Warren Wiersbe says "Unless we understand the distinctive ministry of Paul, we will not fully appreciate the message of God's grace."

Paul clearly lays out 6 Points that characterized his ministry in the passage we are considering today.

Read Romans 15:14-22

What opinion did Paul have of the believers in Rome?

Reread Romans 15:14-16

Read 2 Peter 1: 12

Both Paul and Peter, while having a good opinion of the recipients of their letters, still admonished them. Why did they do this?

Are there times when we as believers, ought to also perform this function to the benefit of other believers? Please give an example.

In verses 15 and 16 how does Paul tell us he received his special duty of going to the Gentiles?

Also Read 1 Corinthians 15:8-10

This then will be the first of:

Six Points That Characterized Paul's Ministry to the Gentiles

1.   THIS DUTY AND PRIVILEGE WAS RECEIVED BY GOD'S GRACE

Read Romans 15:16 again.

What does Paul remind us about regarding the nature of God in this verse? (3)

Read Malachi 1:6-14

What do we learn in this passage about the type of sacrifice that God wants of His people?

Read: 1 Peter 2:5
        Romans 15:16

Viewed together, what do you take these two verses to mean about sacrifice?

What exactly does this sacrifice involve in our lives today?

In rereading Romans 15:16, what was the singular and central focus of what Paul brought to the Gentiles?

This then will become our second point that characterized Paul's ministry to the Gentiles.

2.   It Was Centered In and On the Gospel

Read Romans 15:17-18 again.

What was Paul so enthusiastic about?

What did Paul boast about?

Note: Paul had the opportunity to explain God's plan to people who had no idea about Judaism, the true nature of God, His written Word, or the new life offered by Him.

Read: Jeremiah 9:23-24

     2 Corinthians 10:17-18

At one time or another we must all prepare a resume' and be able to tell others about what we have done in our lives. How can we do this and still be consistent with the above verses?

This then brings us to the third distinctive point that characterized Paul's work.

3.   IT WAS DONE FOR GOD'S GLORY

Read: Ephesians 5:15-16

     Colossians 3:23-24

     Romans 15:18

What other important characteristic of Paul's life do we see highlighted in verse 18?

This, then, brings us to the fourth point that characterized Paul's ministry.

4. He Lived a Consistent Life

How important is it that we each live a consistent life as we act as "salt and light" to the world?

Read: Romans 15:19

> 2 Corinthians 12:12

> Hebrews 2:1-4

Note: The Greek word for "signs" is *semeion,* which means miracles by which God authenticates the men sent by Him, or by which men prove that the cause they are pleading is God's. It also means miracles that signify theological truths.

Note: The Greek word for "wonders" is *teras* which means miracles that produce awe and astonishment.

By what power did Paul advance God's ministry to the Gentiles?

This brings us to the fifth characteristic of Paul's ministry.

5. It Was Done Through God's Power. (The Power of the Holy Spirit)

Read Romans 15:19-22

Does anyone know where Illyricum, mentioned in verse 19, is today?

It was also referred to as Dalmatia and was roughly all the way up in what we call Yugoslavia.

Was it a surprise that Paul's ministry took him on such diverse travels?

Read: Isaiah 52:15

Isaiah 65:1

This brings us to the final point that characterized Paul's ministry.

6. IT WAS ACCORDING TO THE PLAN OF GOD

Trick Question: How many of those in our group today are in "full time ministry?" Please raise your hand.

Application Question

At this point in your life, what can you do to determine whether your vocation (and we all have one) is in line with God's desires for your life?

How does God use you to serve Him through your vocation?

Close in prayer.

Review calendar.

Assign refreshments for next time.

WEEK 32

PAUL'S TRAVEL PLANS AND RELATIONS BETWEEN GENTILE BELIEVERS AND "JEWISH CHRISTIANS"
ROMANS 15: 22-33

Opening Prayer

Group Warm-Up Question:
How do you react when your travel plans are delayed or cancelled? How should you react?

Read Romans 15: 23-33
Where was Paul planning to travel?

What was his planned itinerary?

Was this plan new for him?

Read: Acts 19:21

    Romans 1:9-14

Note: At the time Spain was counted by geographers, such as Strabo, as being at the end of the earth. This was the farthest western end of the Mediterranean and was thought of as being very far away. There was, however, a Roman colony there, where many Jews lived.

According to Strabo, the farthest end of the world on the eastern side was India.

Why was Paul planning to visit Rome? (Think back to Romans 1:9-14)

What special task did Paul need to complete before visiting Rome?

Read: Romans 15:25-26 again.

    1 Corinthians 16:1-3

    2 Corinthians 8:1-5

What impact does giving gifts of this nature have upon the giver?

Read: Philippians 4:15-20

    2 Corinthians 9:12-13

Note: The Greek word used for "contribution" in verse 26 is *koinonian* which literally means "*fellowship, communion, or fiduciary communication.*"

How does your knowledge of the underlying Greek add to your understanding of this passage?

How do these ideas relate to the concept of bearing fruit (not limited to our financial commitments) as seen in John 15:1-8?

Read John 15:1-8 and enumerate what we learn about bearing fruit.

Why did the believers in Greece feel such a debt of obligation to the "Jewish Christians" in Jerusalem?

Read: Romans 15:26-28 again

Reread Romans 15:29-31

What activity needed to go hand-in-hand with sending money to the "Jewish Christians?"

Why was it so important that these two things occur at the same time?

Read: Ephesians 6:19-20

    Colossians 4:3-4

    1 Thessalonians 5:25

    2 Thessalonians 3:1-2

How does this concept of praying for others relate to our lives?

Read Romans 15:31-32 again.

Why was it necessary to pray that the "Jewish Christians" in Jerusalem accepted the gift that Paul was taking to them?

Why do you think that their hoped for acceptance of this gift might make Paul so happy?

Note: Giving money to the poor was already an important part of the laws observed by the Jews. Jewish teachers considered the laws requiring care for the poor to be a major test of whether a Gentile convert to Judaism had genuinely accepted God's law.

Sending money to the poor Jews in Jerusalem (especially to those who were members of the Qumran community who were very, very poor) was a common Jewish practice in the Mediterranean, especially in regard to the annual temple tax. This practice continued among the non-believing Jews at the time of Paul's writing.

In addition to the non-believing Jews, there were many believing Jews in Jerusalem who we referred to as "Jewish Christians" in today's discussion. These believing Jews were often especially impoverished since they were not always recipients of the regional temple tax offerings.

However, even though the believing Jews might have sometimes been in need, there was also a trend among them to act as Judaizers. These Judaizers wanted Gentile converts to first become circumcised.

Remember and Read Romans 2:25-27 for a brief reminder.

Paul knew that it was entirely possible that Jews with this bent might not accept the offering from believing Gentiles who had not been circumcised. Paul prayed that this would not be so since it would be prima facie evidence that the Jews so inclined did not really understand what he said in Romans 2:28-29.

Conversely, if the "Jewish Christians" in Jerusalem accepted the gifts properly, this would indicate that their faith was strong and growing.

Read Galatians 2:1-10 for a quick summary of these concepts in action.

On a historical basis, it is gratifying to note that the believers in Rome did end up giving generously and sacrificially to help poor and suffering believers elsewhere. During the second century they were especially noted for sending funds to needy churches throughout the Roman Empire, and for buying the freedom of Christian slaves from the mines and similar circumstances.

Read Romans 15:33

What exactly do you think Paul was referring to in this verse?

Realizing the privilege we have as noted in Romans 15:33, there is one more thing we need to do.

Application

Read Psalm 90:12

Important thought and question to consider: How many weekends do you have left, and how will you use them?

Today we have read about some of the things first century believers did to help one another. What sacrifice can you make this week to help a believer who is struggling with a burden of some sort?

Remember: How we spend the time, talents, and money we have at our disposal must be properly merged with our time in prayer and God's Word to bear fruit effectively.

Close in prayer.

Review Calendar.

Assign refreshments for next time.

GREETINGS, THANKS, RECOGNITIONS, FINAL SUMMARY AND INSTRUCTIONS
ROMANS 16:1-27

Opening Prayer

Warm-Up Question:

How valuable is a note of thanks, appreciation, and recognition? Why?

Note: This chapter is quite often ignored and neglected by many people as they read the Bible. However, we must remember what we are told in II Timothy 3:16-17. Every part of Scripture is useful for the believer.

Read II Timothy 3:16-17

> 16 "All Scripture is inspired by God and is useful for teaching the truth, rebuking error, correcting faults, and giving instruction for right living,

17 so that the man who serves God may be fully equipped for every
kind of good work."

With that in mind, we cannot ignore this passage. What we hope to do is to learn
some of what God is communicating to us in this last chapter of Romans. It, like
all of Scripture, is there for a purpose as we see in the verses from Timothy that
we just read.

Read Romans 16:1-27

Note: Paul mentions 33 people by name and also refers to many others.

What does the fact that Paul included this long list tell us about the importance
of personal relationships among believers?

Note: Paul knew all these people by name and was aware of their activities and
progress.

For what did Paul recognize Phoebe?

What did he ask the believers in Rome to do for her?

Note: Depending upon the translation you are using you will see Phoebe referred
to as a "servant" or a "deacon." The word in Greek is *diakonon* and is used in the
New Testament for the office of deacon.

Let's take a look at other places this same word is used to get a better idea of just
who Phoebe was and what she was doing. As we read each verse, please relate it
specifically to Phoebe.

Read: Philippians 1:1

1 Timothy 3:8

1 Timothy 3:9

1 Timothy 3:10

1 Timothy 3:11

1 Timothy 3:12

Romans 15:8

1 Corinthians 3:5

For what did Paul recognize Priscilla and Aquilla?

Note: In the United States, most believers have become too complacent about their faith. The Voice of the Martyrs tells us that every year 150,000 believers in Jesus Christ are murdered for their faith. This breaks down to 411 per day, or 17 each hour. These brothers and sisters do not normally receive a clean death. They are most often subject to starvation, torture, rape, and deprivation of the worst kind.

For part of our discussion time today, a timer will go off every 4 minutes. This is simply to remind us that one of our fellow believers has been murdered for engaging in exactly the kind of activity we are doing right now.

Further note on Priscilla and Aquilla: This couple is mentioned many times in the Scriptures. We also see them in:

Acts 18:1-3

Acts 18:18-19

Acts 18:24-28

2 Timothy 4:19

Let's read and discuss these references to get a larger understanding of the good work these particular people were involved with.

What was special about Epenetus?

Why was Mary mentioned?

Why were Andronicus and Junia mentioned? What special distinctions did they have?

What very special comment did Paul make about Apelles?

Note: The Greek words Paul used for "approved" are *ton dokimon,* which means "the one approved through testing; had been put to the test."

What additional special insight does this understanding of the Greek give us into why Apelles received such high approbation? (Approbation is an official expression of warm approval and praise.)

What did Paul have to say about Tryphena, Tryphosa and Persis?

(Note: Some believe that Tryphena and Tryphosa were sisters, perhaps even twins. Their names mean "dainty" and "delicate.")

What does Paul say about Ampliatus?

(Note: In the Domitilla Cemetery, among the catacombs of Rome, there is an ornate grave with the single name, "Ampliatus," an apparent slave. However, the ornateness of the grave suggests he was held in high regard. Many scholars believe this is the same Ampliatus mentioned by Paul in Romans 16:8)

Rufus is mentioned in verse 13. Does anyone remember where else Rufus is mentioned? (See Mark 15:21. Note: Both Mark and Paul assumed everybody knew about Rufus. This was all very recent, very real, up close, and personal to them. They were there. What a thrill and privilege this was.)

Note: In many of these verses Paul recognizes people and those who are "with them." These all seem to be "home churches" or "small groups" if you will (See Romans 16:5, 14, 15, 16, 23).

Note: Although it may be hard to tell because of the types of names these people had, it includes both men and women.

Note: In several places Paul refers to people as his "relatives" or "kinsmen." This seems to be a special reference to believers who were Jews. Both Gentile and Jewish believers were working together.

Historical note: Erastus from Corinth is mentioned in Romans 16:23. Read this one verse again. This was corroborated when a 1929 excavation in Corinth unearthed a pavement with the following words. "ERASTVS PRO:AED: P: STRAVIT" For those of us who can't read Latin this means "Erastus, curator of public buildings, laid this pavement at his own expense."

Let's now read Romans 16:17-18 again.

Why do you think Paul thought this was important enough to include in some of the last lines of his letter to the Romans?

Read: 2 Corinthians 10:4-6

      1 Corinthians 11:1-4

      Philippians 3:17-21

What encouragement did Paul give to those in Rome in Romans 16:19-20? Read these verses again in the King James Version.

Note: The Greek word used for being wise for that which is good is *sophos.* This means "wise, skilled, expert, skilled in letters, learned, cultivated, forming the best plans and using the best means for their execution."

The Greek word for being innocent of any wrong, or simple concerning evil, is *akeraios.* This means "unmixed, pure as in wines or metals, uncontaminated, or in relationship to the mind; without a mixture of evil, free from guile, innocent."

What greater insights do we get from this understanding of the Greek?

What important closing comments did Paul make about God and the Gospel in Romans 16:25-27?

Some Observations about the Early Church

1. They had a real sense of community and love for one another.

2. Life is a battle, a battle to the death.

3. They had a need for rest and leisure. This rest and leisure was not an end
    in itself. It was to better prepare them for and make them more effective
    in the battle.

4. They understood that the gifts of the Spirit provide a special ministry for
    every single believer. (Those that were not using their gifts were short-
    changing God, themselves, their family, other believers, the body of Christ
    as a whole, unbelievers, the society, the culture, the community, and the
    world as a whole. They were not living up to their responsibility in the
    battle if they were not using their gifts. What happens to soldiers who shirk
    their duty in the armed forces?)

Application Questions

How can you remember the seriousness of the life and death battle in which we
as believers are engaged in the world today?

While you are in the midst of this battle, in what specific ways can you show
appreciation to and help other believers?

Pray for our brothers and sisters in Christ around the world who are dying for their
faith and living for our Lord every day. May we take our faith as seriously as they
do, and make a powerful impact upon our immediate world, and the world at large.

Close in prayer.

Review Calendar.

Assign refreshments for next time.

APPENDIX A

HOW TO AVOID ERROR

(Partially excerpted from *The Road to Holocaust* by Hal Lindsey)

1. The most important single principle in determining the true meaning of any doctrine of our faith is that we start with the clear statements of the Scriptures that specifically apply to it, and use those to interpret the parables, allegories and obscure passages. This allows Scripture to interpret Scripture...The Dominionists (and others seeking to bend Scripture to suit their purposes) frequently reverse this order, seeking to interpret the clear passages using obscure passages, parables and allegories.

2. The second most important principle is consistently to interpret by the literal, grammatical, historical method. This means the following:

3. Each word should be interpreted in light of its normal, ordinary usage that was accepted in the times in which it was written.

4. Each sentence should be interpreted according to the rules of grammar and syntax normally accepted when the document was written.

5. Each passage should also be interpreted in light of its historical and cultural environment.

Most false doctrines and heresy of Church history can be traced to a failure to adhere to these principles. Church history is filled with examples of disasters and wrecked lives wrought by men failing to base their doctrine, faith, and practice upon these two principles.

The Reformation, more than anything else, was caused by an embracing of the literal, grammatical, and historical method of interpretation, and a discarding of the allegorical method. The allegorical system had veiled the Church's understanding of many vital truths for nearly a thousand years.

Note 1: It is important to note that this is how Jesus interpreted Scripture. He interpreted literally, grammatically, and recognized double reference in prophecy.

Note 2: It is likewise important that we view Scripture as a whole. Everything we read in God's Word is part of a cohesive, consistent, integrated message system. Every part of Scripture fits in perfectly with the whole of Scripture if we read, understand, and study it properly.

Note 3: Remember to Appropriate the power of The Holy Spirit.

Read: Luke 11:11-12

    Luke 24:49

    John 7:39

    John 14:14-17, 26

    1Timothy 4: 15-16

    2 Peter 2: 1

    Mark 13: 22

APPENDIX B

STILL CHOSEN WITH ADDITIONAL SCRIPTURE REFERENCES

1. Romans 11:17-18—Israel is the Root. (Romans 11:18 in the NLT makes it particularly clear that the church does not replace Israel.)

2. Matthews 10:5-6—Gospel First to the Jews

3. John 4:22—Salvation comes through the Jews.

4. Acts 1:16—Jesus infers the future return of the land to the Jews but says it will be on His timetable.

5. Acts 2: and Acts 3:1-4:4—Peter, Apostle to the Jews

6. Acts 10: 1, 2—Peter to a Roman Officer, halfway Jewish Convert?

7. Acts 10:27-29, 34-35, 44-45—Peter to the Gentiles.

8. Acts 11:2-3, 9-18—Peter criticized for Gentile ministry, and explanation.

9. Acts 11:19—Stephen preaching only to the Jews.

10. Acts 11: 26—Jewish converts first called Christians. Paul always went to the Synagogue to preach.

11. Genesis 17:7-8—Abrahamic Covenant relative to the Jews as a people and the land.

12. Deuteronomy 4:32-40—Speaks of the land God gave the Jews for all time.

13. Deuteronomy 7:6—God's unique choosing of the Jews.

14. Deuteronomy 30:3-5—Prophecy of return to the land even if dispersed.

15. Leviticus 26:14-45—God chastises Jews and yet still keeps His promise.

16. Leviticus 26:44-45—God honors his covenant even in the midst of disobedience.

17. Jeremiah 31:35-37—God will not abandon Jews.

18. Jeremiah 33:24-26—God remains faithful to His covenant with the Jews.

19. Psalms 89:19-37—God does not abandon Jews even in face of disobedience, though they still are accountable and must bear consequences.

20. Romans 11:1-2—Paul speaking to the error of replacement theology.

21. Hebrews 8:7-9—Consequences of breaking the Mosaic Covenant.

22. 2 Timothy 3:16-17—All Scripture's Inspired. At the time this referred to the Old Testament and that is how it was understood.

23. Romans 11:23-24—Jews to be grafted back in.

24. 1 Corinthians 10:32—Paul referencing humanity in three parts, Jews, Gentiles, the Church.

25. Romans 3:1-2—God's word committed to the Jews.

26. Romans 3:3—God's promise to the Jews is irrevocable even if they are not faithful.

27. Genesis 12:3—"I will bless them that bless thee, and curse him that curseth thee." Reciprocal Blessing.

28. Genesis 12—A series of 7 unilateral promises.

29. Amos 9:15—Promise of return to the land. Also alluded to in Romans 9:4.

30. Romans 11:18—Gentiles not to boast since they are grafted in.

31. Romans 1:16—Paul considers Jews primary candidates of Salvation.

32. Romans 15:26-27—Gentile churches urged to financially support the mother Jewish Church in the land of Israel.

33. Romans 11:28-29—God's call to and choosing of Israel never withdrawn. Paul's reference to True Jews was made to Jews who needed completion. A True Jew is one who is physically a Jew and spiritually renewed. A gentile cannot become a True Jew.

34. 1 Corinthians 5:7-8—Why Christians should observe the Passover.

35. Jewish Believers might well ask, "How can a Gentile be saved?"

36. Psalms 121:4—He who watches over Israel never tires and never sleeps.

37. Proverbs 30:6—Do not add to his words, or he may rebuke you and you may be found a liar.

38. Revelation 2:9, 3:9—False Jews

39. Revelation 22: 18-20—Warning against removing or adding words to God's revelation.

40. Daniel 11:28-30—Speaks of the People of the Holy Covenant.

41. Luke 1:73—God remembers the oath he swore to bless all peoples through Abraham.

42. 2 Samuel 23:5—God's blessing to come through David's line.

43. Isaiah 11—Says when Israel is gathered in the Promised Land the second time, they will not be removed. (See verses 11-12)

44. John 10:35—The Scriptures cannot be altered.

45. Matthew 25—People measured by how they treat Jesus' "brothers" referring to the Jews.

46. **The name Israel appears 73 times in the New Testament and each time refers to the nation of Israel and not to some allegorical concept of a replacement nation made up of a church of Gentiles.**

47. **No other race has endured a more concentrated onslaught by the enemies of God to wipe it off of the face of the earth.**

48. Jeremiah 31:36—Israel as an enduring and everlasting national entity.

49. Jeremiah 31:8—Regathering.

50. Ezekiel 38 and 39—God says Gog and Magog will come up against His people (Israel) who are on His Land.

51. Matthew 10: 5-6—Jesus sent his disciples out to see the Jews.

52. Galatians 3:15-29—Relates to God's promise, which cannot be lost, and relates it to the law.

53. Galatians 3:20—Now a mediator is needed if two people enter into an agreement, but God acted on his own when He made his promise to Abraham.

54. Galatians 6:16—Refers to believers in Israel and not to the church.

55. Ephesians 2:12—Says that the Gentiles did not know the promises God made to the Jews.

56. Revelation 2:9 and 3:9—Both refer to "those who claim to be Jews but are not." Some commentators say this refers to those who proclaim replacement theology.

57. Isaiah 41: 8-9—Status of being chosen is not negated by temporary waywardness.

58. Isaiah 54:10—Their place in God's plan is not changed even though they were disobedient.

59. Isaiah 66:22—You will always be my people.

60. Ezekiel 20:33-38—Regathering

61. Ezekiel 36:8-10, 22 24—Regathering

62. Isaiah 43: 6 Regathering

63. Psalms 89—Not Finished with Israel

64. Answering anyone thinking God has abandoned his promises to Israel because no one is on David's Throne:

    • Revelation 4:5—Jesus is on the Throne.

    • Isaiah 11:10—Jesus is heir to the Throne.

    • Isaiah 9:7—Jesus is heir.

    • Isaiah 16:4-5—A faithful king will reign who always does what is just and right. (Jesus Christ)

65. Scripture is replete with references to Jesus prior to and after his coming. Where does he sit?

- Hebrews 12:2

- Acts 17:7

- John 19:19

- Mark 15:32

- Romans 8:34

- Revelation 1:5

- Revelation 19:16

- Revelation 17:14

- Colossians 3:1

- Ephesians 1:20

66. Isaiah 66:22—They will always be my people.

APPENDIX C

MATHEMATICAL PROPHECY OF THE RETURN OF ISRAEL
MAY 14, 1948

The Judeo Christian Scriptures and the truths contained therein are reliable beyond any doubt. The can be and is verified by a correct application of some of what we call the sciences as well as *all* other sources of study. This is true of archaeology, psychology, medicine, history, and surprising to some, mathematics.

In this material we have read about the reestablishment of Israel as a nation. This occurred on May 14, 1948. The most amazing part of this is that if one examines the prophecies in the Tanakh and adjusts them correctly for changing calendars we find that the exact day of this Historic event was foretold to the day about 2,500 years earlier.

For an in-depth review of the mathematical calculations involved in analyzing this prophecy you may wish to take a look at http://alphanewsdaily.com/mathprophecy2.html.

It is not necessary, however, to go through these mathematical machinations in order to understand that this particular event and those surrounding it have been part of God's plan all along. We see that clearly in an honest reading of the biblical text as referenced in Appendix B.

BIBLIOGRAPHY

REFERENCES UTILIZED IN THE PREPARATION OF THIS MATERIAL

Anderson, Ken, *What Does the Bible Say About*, Nashville, Tennessee, Thomas Nelson Publishers, 2001.

Anderson, Ken, *Where to Find it in the Bible*, Nashville Tennessee, Thomas Nelson, 2004.

Beale, G. K. and D. A. Carson, Editors, *Commentary on the New Testament Use of the Old Testament*, Grand Rapids, Michigan, Baker Academic, 2007.

Behe, Michael J., *Darwin's Black Box*, New York, London, Toronto, Sidney, Free Press, 2006.

Briesbach, Daniel L. and Mark David Hall editors, *The Sacred Rights of Conscience*, Indianapolis, Indiana, Liberty Fund, Inc., 2009.

Bullinger, E. W., *Number in Scripture*, Grand Rapids, Michigan, Kregel Publications, 1967.

Cleveland, William, *A History of the Modern Middle East*, Boulder, Colorado, Oxford, England, Westview Press, 2008.

Collins, Larry, and Dominique LaPierre, *O'Jerusalmem*, New York, London, Toronto, Sydney, Simon & Schuster, 2007.

Comfort, Roy, *God Doesn't Believe in Atheists: Proof That the Atheist Doesn't Exist*, Gainesville, Florida, Bridge Logos Publishers, 1993.

Denton, Micahel, *Evolution: Theory in Crisis*, Chevy Chase, Maryhland, Adler & Adler, 1986.

Dershowitz, Alan, *The Case For Israel*, Hoboken, New Jersey, John Wiley & Sons, Inc., 2003.

Eternal Publications, *Scientific Facts and Foreknowledge*

Eternal Publications, *Last Days Prophecies (101)*

Evans, Mike, *Jerusalem Betrayed*, Dallas Texas, Word Publishing, 1997.

Gordon-Conwell Theological Seminary, *The Archaeological Study Bible, Grand Rapids*, Michigan, Zondervan, 2005

Green, Jay P. Sr., Translator, *Hebrew-Greek English Interlinear Bible*, Authors for Christ, Lafayette, Indiana, 2000.

Hunt, David, *A Cup of Trembling*, Eugene, Oregon, Harvest House Publishers, 1995.

Intervarsity Press, *New Testament Lesson Planner*, Colorado Springs, Colorado, 1992.

Joffe, Gerardo, *Facts and Logic About the Middle East*, factsandlogic.org. San Francisco, California, 2009.

Johnson, Phillip E., *Darwinism on Trial*, Downers Grove, Illinois, IVP Books, 1993.

Keener, Craig S., *The Bible Background (New Testament) Commentary from IVP*, Downers Grove, Illinois, IVP Academic, 1993.

Lewis, David, *Can Israel Survive in a Hostile World*, Green, Forest, Arizona, New Leaf Press, 1994.

Lindsey, Hal, *The Road to Holocaust*, New Your, New York, Bantam Books 1989.

Lotus, John and Mark Aarons, *The Secret War Against the Jews*, New York, New York, St. Martin's Grifin, 1997.

Logos Research Systems, *Scholars Library Silver Edition*, CD-ROM, Bellinham Waxhington, 2004.

McDowell, Josh, *The New Evidence That Demands a Verdict (Volumes I and II)*, Nashville, Tennessee, Thomas Nelson, 1999.

McTiernan, John, *As America Has Done to Israel*, New Kensington, Pennsylvania, Whitaker House, 2008.

Missler, Charles, *Betrayal of the Chosen*, Audio Cassette, Coueur d' Alene, Idaho, Koinonia Houjse, 1997.

Missler, Charles and Nancy Missler, *Be Ye Transformed*, Coureur d' Alene, Idaho, King's Highway Ministries, 2009.

Missler, Charles, *Koinonia House Commentary on Romans*, Coeur d' Alene, Idaho, Koinonia House, 1999.

Missler, Charles, *The Prodigal Heirs: Israel and the Church*, Audio Cassete, Coueur d' Alene, Idaho, Koinonia House, 1995.

Netanyahu, Benjamin, *A Place Among the Nations*, New York, New York, Bantam Books, 1993.

Peters, Joan, *From Time Immemorial*, Chicago, Illinois, JKAP Publications, 2001.

Ridolfi, Brian, *What Does the Bible Say About*, Chattanooga, Tennessee, AMG Publishers, 2005

Richards, Jay and Guillermo Gonzalez, *The Privileged Planet: How Our Place in the Cosmos is Designed for Discovery*, Book and DVD, Washinton, CD, Regency Publishing 2004.

Shirer, William, *The Rise and Fall of The Third Reich*, New York, London, Toronto, Tokyo, Sydney, Singapore, Simon & Schuster, 1990.

Stoner, Peter W., *Scientce Speaks*, Chicago, Illinois, Moody Press, 1963.

Wiersbe, Warren W. *The Wiersbe Bible Commentary: The Complete New Testament in One Volume*, Colorado Springs, CO, David C. Cook, 2007.

Wiersbe, Warren W., *The Wiersbe Bible Commentary: The Complete Old Testament in One Volume,* Colorado Springs, CO, David C. Cook, 2007.

Wildersmith, A. E., *Man's Origin; Man's Destiny*, Bethan House Publisheres, 1968,

Young, Robert, *Young's Analytical Concordance to the Bible*, Grand Rapids, Michigan, W. B. Eerdmans Publishing Company, 1970.

ABOUT THE AUTHOR

Fred Scheeren, Managing Director-Investments with one of the world's largest financial companies has achieved a distinguished career by putting his client's interests first. He has been a practicing Certified Financial Planner™ for over 25 years and was one of the first to receive that designation.

He was included in the 2005, 2008, 2009,2010, 2012, 2012, 2013, and 2014 editions of "Guide to America's Best Financial Planners" and was also included in the Barron's (a publication of the Wall Street Journal) Top 1000 Advisors in 2009 2010, 2011, 2012 and 2013. In 2014 he was included in the expanded Barron's Top 1200 Advisors.

He received the Securities Industry Institute's top award at the University of Pennsylvania's prestigious Wharton School of Business in the 1980's for his analysis of the securities industry. He has twice been named to Who's Who in Business and Finance among Financial Advisors and has regularly conducted continuing education seminars for legal and accounting professionals. He has served as the primary speaker on investment strategy for the Society of CPA's, the State Bar Association, the State Medical Association, and the Social Security Administration in WV.

Utilizing the analytical skills which have made him successful in his profession, Mr. Scheeren has presented a number of 10 week programs on Islam, Israel, and the Church to a number of churches in various denominations. In addition, he has presented numerous Bible Studies to groups of various sizes over the course of the last 40 years.

Mr. Scheeren and his wife, Sally, an attorney in private practice and a Messianic Jew, have four grown boys and three grandchildren.